Unstoppable Church

Embracing God's development plan

Hugh Osgood

malcolm down
PUBLISHING

First published 2024 by Malcolm Down Publishing Ltd.
www.malcolmdown.co.uk

28 27 26 25 24   7 6 5 4 3 2 1

British Library Cataloguing in Publication Data
A catalogue record for this book is available from the British Library.

ISBN: 978-1-915046-80-2

Cover design by Angela Selfe
Art direction by Sarah Grace

Printed in the UK.

Typeset using Atomik ePublisher from Easypress Technologies.

Acknowledgements

This book emerged from my Honest Theology podcast. When I decided to look at discipleship with director and filmmaker Paul Syrstad, we needed to be sure our ideas lined up enough to make for a useful debate. After a lot of walking and talking, we came up with the idea of a book that used my early years of ministry to set out some of the things we discussed. While this book draws on illustrations from my twenties and thirties, Paul is still enjoying his. It would never have been written without his provocation and encouragement.

Contents

Foreword

There are many words that we could use to describe Hugh. He's a deep-thinking theologian, a powerful preacher, a caring family man, a visionary apostle, a creative church planter and, I'd imagine, a competent dentist – although I never had the chance to prove it! But the word that flows out of this book is that Hugh is first and foremost a disciple of Jesus.

Unstoppable Church is an invitation to a ringside view of Hugh's early journey as a disciple and church leader. He draws on his personal experiences, sharing honestly and profoundly the joys and the challenges of being involved in God's great story. But more than just his personal story, he masterfully weaves in the New Testament narrative, to help us recognise the lessons that the early Church has for us today.

The word 'disciple' can be translated as 'learner'. And as Hugh reflects in the rearview mirror of his life, we see that in every season there are things that God wants to teach us and reveal to us. Hugh is always learning, and there is a humility in this book that is evident in Hugh's life as he has inputted into my life and so many others.

As I've devoured this book, two words really spring to mind about the discipleship journey that we are each invited on. The first is *intentional*.

We can each have grandiose plans for our lives and ideas of what we'd like to do for God. But Hugh's story and biblical reflections remind us again and again of the importance of intentionally submitting to God.

We can look for the perfect discipleship programme to work through and apply in our lives and in our churches, but the truth that reverberates from the pages of *Unstoppable Church* is that discipleship isn't ultimately about a course we do but about a life we live, intentionally seeking God. The principles in this book powerfully demonstrate the practical necessity of soaking ourselves in Scripture and inviting God to lead us.

The second word is *relational*. This book is ultimately about relationships. It's about Hugh's relationship with God and his relationship with co-pilgrims. It's through relationships that often God speaks and it's through relationships that the Church flourishes.

Unstoppable Church is a reminder of the importance of investing time in others and grasping that we get to play a part in a much bigger story that spans the nations of the world and the pages of history.

I am so thankful to Hugh for all he has done on so many levels to build the Church in London, the UK and around the globe, but most of all, I am thankful that Hugh is a disciple of Jesus who has modelled to me and so many others what it means to be intentional in seeking God and building relationships. Enjoy the read!

Andy Frost
Joint CEO, Gather Movement

Introduction

Someone once came to me with a dreamy look in their eye and said, 'I believe God's calling me to speak to thousands.' As they imagined the stadium, the lights, the amplification system and the high-profile personalities on the platform, a lateral thought sprang into my mind and I found myself saying, 'And what if God sends them to you one at a time?'

Right now, I want to turn that question around. Many of us would never dream that we could, or even should, speak from such a vast platform. We feel far more secure being tucked away in a crowd than we ever would standing in front of one. In Bible terms, we're more inclined to see ourselves as one of the 5,000 rather than one of the Twelve. But, here's the question: 'What if God is actually calling us one at a time?'

As we let this sink in, we need to remind ourselves that God is definitely into crowds – he can handle thousands upon thousands. Yet it's possible that everyone in a crowd he gathers can have a clear sense of personal calling, as if he were addressing them on their own. If we're right, then every one of the 3,000 in the crowd who responded at Pentecost could have heard the call to follow Jesus just as clearly as each of the Twelve. I believe that's not only possible, but from God's point of view, it's absolutely essential. How else could he express the reality of his loving concern and commitment as he brings us into a discipleship relationship with himself? When the Holy Spirit is breathing new life into us, he is at the same time confirming us in our new relationship with God the Father as his children, and with Jesus as his disciples. As

Peter preached 'everyone who calls on the name of the Lord will be saved' (Acts 2:21),[1] there was a matching call in their hearts from the Lord Jesus – 'follow me' (Matthew 4:19; Mark 1:17). Becoming disciples was part of the joy of their salvation at Pentecost and it is part of the joy of our salvation today too.

But as Peter and Andrew, James and John, and the others who'd been called earlier were already discovering, being a disciple of Jesus is not just about following, or cosying up smugly into a new relationship. When Jesus called them, it was a case of 'Follow Me, and I will make you ...' (Matthew 4:19, NKJV).

Now, before I write 'fishers of men' (Matthew 4:19, NKJV), some of you may already have some ideas of your own about what he's making you into: a shepherd of his sheep, a fisher of people, a teacher, a preacher, a challenger, an administrator, a friend, an encourager? But let's not be too hasty. Making predictions can be a way of setting up limitations. He may be calling you to be some of those things, or may even be calling you to be all of those things, and yet at times he could still be telling you: 'I want you right now to just stop and be a silent worshipper – "lost in wonder, love, and praise".'[2] We've all been called in order to be 'made ...', having a personal calling to follow the risen Jesus so he can make us into what he wants us to be. This will be more than we can imagine[3] – a blessing to him and a blessing to others.

So, having called us one by one, he now has to introduce us to his training programme that will work for us all. Churches often try to implement discipleship programmes while overlooking the fact that God has already designed his own amazing discipleship plan to make sure we all grow and all grow together. It's his Church.

---

1. See Joel 2:32.
2. Charles Wesley (1707-88), https://hymnary.org/text/love_divine_all_love_excelling_joy_of_he (accessed 11.12.23).
3. See Ephesians 3:20.

Of course, having designed a 'one-size-fits-all' plan doesn't prevent God from working it out differently in different places. After all, God is infinitely creative, so it's inevitable that his global Church will always be incredibly diverse. It has to be, in order to be locally relevant in an endlessly diverse world. I've come to believe that it will take the whole Church to reach the whole of society. It's not enough for us to say, 'If my church gets it right, it'll change everything.' We all need to take God's discipleship principles to heart – to share in his life, to commit to his plan, to relate to one another and grow.

There isn't a church that I know of that isn't keen to get it right. And yet we can be quite ungenerous to one another in our assessments. When John wrote the book of Revelation, he knew that all seven churches in his local area had come up against major problems in their first three to four decades of existence.[4] The depth of concern that Jesus showed in addressing them would have come as no surprise to John. But he might have been surprised to know that many today assume that five of those churches must have quickly ceased to exist. Perhaps such pessimism runs deeper than we think, leaving us discouraged about our own church as well as the churches attended by others. Some of those churches around John had massive problems, but he had seen Jesus standing in the middle of them,[5] giving each an accurate diagnosis, a clear prescription and an encouraging promise that would enable things to change.[6] Why don't we assume that love, grace and truth could have turned them around and lifted them to a higher place? Updating our thinking and standing with one another in a spirit of encouragement should be easy in the light of this. Jesus stood with seven churches, committed to seeing love and life restored, corruption, compromise

---

4. Revelation 1 – 3.
5. Revelation 1:12-13.
6. Revelation 2:1 – 3:22.

and apathy removed, and flickering flames strengthened. Let's make no mistake about it, Jesus is committed to his Church.[7]

I too am passionate about seeing our churches, and us as individuals, rise to higher levels. If the Church is God's discipleship plan, then let's see our local congregations and our denominations become as effective as possible at implementing that plan to the benefit of us all. And if that happens, those of us who are committed to our congregations and denominations won't be the only ones to benefit. Society at large – the communities that surround our churches – will benefit too. I know that life is essential for growth, but so are learning, relating, committing, inspiring and shouldering responsibility. It's these things together that make up God's 'whole church' discipleship plan, and it's as we implement these congregation by congregation, denomination by denomination, church by church that we'll discover that what God has designed works for us individually as well as for all.

Some may want to label what I'm about to set out as a 'lay mobilisation programme'. That's fine. Others will recognise that there is a strong focus on defining leadership in the pages that follow. And that shouldn't come as a surprise. After all, the Twelve with whom Jesus first implemented this discipleship plan were all heading into leadership roles, and the plan works best when we keep this in mind. But we shouldn't restrict 'leadership learned in church' to 'leadership that must be exercised in church'. Of course, the Church needs its leaders in place – to share the load, to inspire and to attract. But everyone who leads within the Church should be serving as a role model, whether they are using their ministry gifts to equip by example or creating space for everyone else through their oversight and servant-heartedness. They should be leaders among leaders.

To help set out how all of this can happen, I'll use examples from the

---

7. Matthew 16:18.

Church in New Testament times, as well as some from my own experience with a church in south London that grew from almost nothing. In doing this, I'm trusting that you won't think I'm advocating simplicity, newness or smallness. God's discipleship plan is about liberation, so it wouldn't make any sense at all to get hung up on structure, age, or size. Being complicated, old and large could even have more advantages than being simple, new and small. That said, I am grateful to all in south London who helped shape me.

What I have written in this book should be particularly useful for anyone getting to grips with 'whole church' discipleship in a local, community-based setting. Interestingly, this is where the vast majority of churches function, and where I was focused in my twenties and thirties. I later went on to develop 'whole church' discipleship in a city-wide resource-centre church and a church at the heart of a network.

To make sure that what I have written here is accessible to those in their twenties and thirties, I have written with a close friend in that age bracket. But please don't think that what I have written is only applicable to twenty- and thirty-year-olds. It will work for anyone, not least for those who lead churches and are willing to learn alongside their congregation, being prepared to see themselves as within the church they lead rather than above it, beneath it or beyond it.

I trust you'll find making this discipleship journey with me exciting and inspiring.

Chapter One: Living Stones

I want you to imagine a man building a wall. He has his bricks. He has his mortar. He has his trowel. And he lays everything out beautifully. He's building row upon row. Then he stands back to admire his work and suddenly everything changes. The bricks are moving and shifting all by themselves. They're alive. They're becoming different shapes and sizes. Some are outgrowing others, and that regular wall doesn't look perfect any more. The builder is exasperated. No one wants the trouble of building with living stones.

Except that isn't really true. Because building with 'living stones' is exactly what Jesus has determined to do (1 Peter 2:4-5).

It's a hot afternoon in Caesarea Philippi, some distance from where Jesus lives. He's arrived with his disciples. They're tired. They're dusty, and he suddenly starts asking questions. He says to them, 'Who do people say I am?' and they come up with different answers. Some have heard people say 'Jeremiah'. Some have heard 'Elijah'. Some have heard 'John the Baptist … risen from the dead' (Matthew 14:2). But then Jesus turns it around and says, 'Who do you say I am?' And Peter says, 'You are the Messiah, the Son of the living God' (Matthew 16:13-16). And that is the trigger. It enables Jesus to say, 'This was not revealed to you by flesh and blood, but by my Father in heaven … and on this rock I will build my church, and the gates of Hades will not overcome it' (Matthew 16:17-18).

Jesus is building an unconquerable, indestructible, unstoppable Church, and the reason it is all of these things is because he's building it with living stones.

Now, I don't know about you, but I clearly remember the shift I went through from being a dead stone to a living one. It's different for each one of us, but my story goes something like this.

When I went to university, I was challenged by the Christian Union to join in their meetings. I was already leading a youth group in an Anglican church, and I'd sort of got quite interested in the intellectual side of Christianity. In fact, before I went to university, I thought I needed to make myself look more 'intellectually astute'. No one in my family had been to university and no one in my school had either. I had no idea what I was going into. I just thought I needed to look clever, so I went completely overboard and decided to read through the theological section in the local library. It was way over my head. And when I got to university, I discovered that all it had done was to make me incredibly judgemental. I'd get invited to a Christian meeting and when people prayed, I would be judging their prayers and not really participating in any way at all. But, despite the fact that I didn't think those prayers were great, they pursued me right into that first summer holiday from university and I just couldn't get away from the fact that somehow God was on my case.

I went walking with a friend in the Lake District. The scenery was fantastic. One day as we walked past a shop in a small town, a postcard caught my eye. It had a picture of the Keswick Convention tent with a sign above it that read 'All one in Christ Jesus'. I remember reacting and thinking, 'Who'd want to buy a card like that? All one in Christ Jesus!' But the phrase wouldn't get out of my mind.

My friend knew something of my restlessness, and tried to think of books he'd read that might help me. I guess he thought I needed some kind of confidence boost. So, as he was a county-level runner, he lent me a book on middle-distance running. It was written by someone who was a well-known coach. He'd trained Olympic athletes. And one of the athletes had sent him a letter – it was a tribute letter. And because he wanted to honour his coach, he had decided to mention one of his coach's heroes on every page. Jesus was included, but was in the middle of the list. Now, again, I don't know why this affected me so much but I remember thinking, 'You can't put Jesus in the middle of a list – he has to be at the top or you just don't mention him at all.'

I was trying to sort out my head and my heart, but it was a real struggle.

I found myself drawn to theology again but I didn't want to re-read the theological section in the library, so I bought a copy of *Mere Christianity* by C.S. Lewis,[1] and a few books on the evidence for the resurrection. These were great and began to sort out my head. But, in the end, my heart was challenged by two little tracts, short books that had been written by a new vicar who'd moved into our area. Who would have thought, after all that I'd read, it would be two small booklets that really hit home? But hit home they did. So much so that I found myself kneeling by my bed and saying, 'God, I want you to do something in my life. If you've been raised from the dead, I want to know something of your resurrection power.'

I prayed that prayer for a few days. I didn't have much faith, but sure enough, something was happening. There was a moment when I was walking home from a piano lesson when, seemingly from nowhere, I found myself remembering a song I'd been taught as a child in Sunday school. It said: 'Things are different now, something happened to me when I gave my heart to Jesus. Things I loved before have passed away, things I love far more have come to stay.'[2] No sooner had this gone through my mind than I stopped stock still. I could take you to the spot on the pavement where it happened. The realisation just exploded

1. C.S. Lewis, *Mere Christianity* (London: Collins, 2012).
2. 'Things are different now', Stanton W. Gavitt. Copyright © 1941 New Spring Publishing Inc. (ASCAP) (adm. At CapitolCMGPublishing.com) All rights reserved. Used by permission.

in my head. 'It's true. Things *are* different now.' The struggle between my head and my heart had gone. The turmoil had given way to a new calmness and confidence. It might not have been my first encounter with God, but it certainly was a big shift in my life. Looking back, it was clear that this dead stone had come to life.

And if I needed any more evidence, I just knew in that moment that my attitude to people had changed. I felt differently towards Christians known to me in the area. And although I'd previously reached the point where I wanted to distance myself from Christians at university, I now couldn't wait to get back to meet up with them all. It was exciting. I just wanted to be with Christians, and I hadn't ever felt like that before. A verse in the Bible from John's first letter says, 'We know that we have passed from death to life, because we love each other' (1 John 3:14). I now knew that I'd found that life.

Now, I don't know what it was like for you. You might have grown up with a steady Christian faith and had just one moment when suddenly you realised that you'd committed your life to Christ in a way that was a real heart response, rather than just a commitment to the Church or a system. Perhaps you came to him, as I did, with a sense of brokenness, no longer trusting in myself but trusting in him. And you found it changed everything.

Or it could have been that you were at an evangelistic event and there was a moment when the evangelist called you to the front to pray a prayer of repentance and faith. They then told you that you were now part of God's family and that there are four things you had to do: 'You need to learn, so you must read your Bible; you need to grow, so you must join with other Christians; you need to pray, so you must speak to God; and you need to share your faith, so you must talk to others.'

But the interesting thing to me, if you'll come with me on a journey back to the Day of Pentecost, is when the Church began… Peter stood up and preached an amazing evangelistic message... he gave a great appeal... he asked people to respond, saying that they needed to repent and be baptised to see their sins washed away... he made it clear that there was a promise of a new life with Jesus that was for them and their children and those who were yet a long way off... and 3,000 people responded, all being baptised.[3] But he never said, 'You need to learn, so you must read your Bible; you need to grow, so you must join with other Christians; you need to pray, so you must speak to God; and you need to share your faith, so you must talk to others.' It wasn't necessary because it seems that the desire to do these things had come as part of the package.[4] They knew from day one that doing all of this made perfect sense.

I can't imagine that it was a case of 'Tomorrow morning you're to gather at Solomon's Colonnade so that we, the apostles, can teach you'. I don't think the Twelve ever saw it that way, not even for a moment. They weren't trying to make their own disciples. They wanted everyone to be a disciple of Jesus. I think it's far more likely that the 3,000 were saying to Peter and the rest of the Twelve, 'You know a lot more than we do. Can you meet with us and teach us? We'll be here in Solomon's Colonnade tomorrow praying with each other, and it would be great if you could come and share with us everything you know, so that we can tell as many people as possible.'[5] If these things were there in their hearts, they didn't have to be told to do them. How powerful must that have been?

So, I can well understand the exasperation of our imaginary builder. But as I stand back and look at the Church, I am more fascinated than exasperated. What an amazing thing Jesus is doing. How stupendous it

---

3. Acts 2:14-41.
4. Acts 2:42-47.
5. Acts 5:12-14.

is that he can build with living stones and how exciting it is that I have become one of them. I'm sure you feel the same.

Now the big question is, how does Jesus do it? How exactly does he fit us all together?

Question for reflection

How important is it for everyone who wants to be part of the Church Jesus came to build to have a personal encounter with God?

Chapter Two: Growing Together

There's a world-famous marathon that starts in a park near where I live. Thousands of people join in, so they have to set off at different times. This could make spotting the winner rather tricky, but most people don't go into the race to win. A lot of them take part to improve on the time it took them last year. They each have their own goal but enjoy running in a group so they can set the pace for each other.

Now, this is a really helpful picture for us as Christians. Paul describes the Christian life as a race,[6] and we can see that when we're looking for inspiration, we needn't just focus on the one who is tipped to win, but we can look around at the people who are more at our level and likely to run at our speed.[7] So often in church life it seems that instead of all running together we try to divide people up. We see some as experts and some as beginners, often categorising people even before the race has got going. It's even become quite usual to take the new people in the church away from the people that brought them, so as to put them with an 'expert'. This can be pretty intimidating, given that in no way can they possibly be all at the same kind of level.

I've become a great believer in running this race together: all determined to reach the goal, encouraging one another, aiming to improve as much as we can, and grateful for the inspiration from those around us as well as from those almost out of sight, running flat out into the distance.

---

6. 1 Corinthians 9:24-26; Hebrews 12:1; 2 Timothy 2:5; 4:7.
7. Hebrews 10:24.

So, let's think about how this worked out in the ministry of Jesus. I really do believe that Jesus was quite deliberate in gathering crowds and teaching everyone at once. But this didn't stop individuals from feeling special. If we think about John for a moment, he certainly considered himself to be the one 'whom Jesus loved' (John 21:7), but in reality he knew that Jesus loved everybody.[8] It would not have been lost on him that when Jesus sent people out in twos there was never a possibility of Jesus saying 'and by the way, I'm going to go with John.'[9] No, John had to go with everyone else, and serve as part of the team, or just accept being part of a crowd in which everyone felt really valued. And although at times Jesus gave special instruction to the Twelve when they were together,[10] he never said when faced with a crowd, 'Now, you guys don't need to listen to this because I'm going to talk to the people who haven't yet heard it.' The overriding principle was that everyone had to listen to everything.[11]

All of this fits in with the fact that Jesus was teaching his disciples to *be* disciples and to *make* disciples. He wasn't teaching them to *have* disciples. They had to accept that everyone who was gathering was being gathered to him. So after the Ascension, when the Spirit of God came on the Day of Pentecost, and not only changed the lives of 120 in the upper room but of 3,000 in the public square below,[12] there would have been a tremendous commitment to all journeying on together in the life they'd just set out to live. The apostles wouldn't have been insisting 'we're out front in this race and you have to catch up'. Of course they knew more than most and wanted to share what

---

8. 1 John 4:9-10.
9. Luke 10:1.
10. Mark 4:10-11.
11. Matthew 11:15; Mark 4:9,23.
12. Acts 2:1-41.

they knew,[13] but they also understood that they were still learning from Jesus and from one another, and that everyone else would now be learning from Jesus and from one another too. It was all about a real sense of oneness.

Yes, the apostles were special, but they were careful not to divide the early Church into experts and beginners. They never insisted that certain things could only happen if they were present, or that things had to be done differently when they were there. This kind of togetherness is a real mark of an unstoppable church.[14]

Now, given all of this, it was really exciting for me, once I'd joined the race and gone back to university for my second year, to discover that this kind of togetherness that was evident in the ministry of Jesus was right at the heart of the Christian Union which I'd been trying so hard to avoid in my first year. There were people in the background travelling around the universities to make sure that we were all doing well, but they left plenty of space for us to learn as equals. We chose the speakers and the topics. We planned together, and counselled and encouraged one another in our coffee breaks and lunch breaks. Rather than always looking to experts, we were prepared to be pacesetters for one another.[15] Sometimes I'd be ahead of my friends and sometimes my friends would be ahead of me. And I think that's just the way it should be; even if my friend came to Jesus more recently than I did, what did that matter? We could still learn from one another. That's why for me the marathon is such a powerful picture.

So, with this kind of peer mentoring in mind, let's think about role models and competitiveness. Paul was a trailblazer and encouraged people to 'follow my example, as I follow the example of Christ'

---

13. Acts 2:42-43.
14. Acts 2:44-47.
15. Hebrews 10:24.

(1 Corinthians 11:1). He also urged people to run the race so as to win.[16] And it's good to put these two things into perspective. Having role models is great but it is not good to idolise them, even if we do marvel at how confidently they race away so far ahead of us. We need to remember that they too are disciples of Jesus and that they're still learning, as we are. Maybe they could even learn from us, since the Bible talks about how we can benefit from each other's input.[17] And what about competitiveness? Well, I for one would be really disappointed if we all tried to run this race at the speed of the slowest. That would mean the only person who'd really put in their best effort would be the person who would have come last, and I'm sure even they would have improved their time if someone had run faster ahead of them. So, there's nothing wrong with running to win unless you end up putting down other people because you don't think they're as good as you are.[18] That's when competitiveness becomes a snare.

So, my plea is this. Let's do 'whole church' discipleship. Let's be more mature and do a lot less picking and a lot more mixing. As students, if we'd booked an evangelistic speaker, we were all there to listen. If we'd asked someone to speak on discipleship, we were all there to hear. If we'd decided on a mini theological lecture, we were all there for that too. We were all taking part in the same race, all wanting to improve, all believing that the more we gave of ourselves the more we'd grow.

Now, this all may sound great and some of you might even call it idealistic, and I could agree up to a point. Nonetheless, it's what we strove for and I believe it's what the early Church knew. But if your experience has been anything like mine, you'll know that knockbacks are coming.

---

16. 1 Corinthians 9:24.
17. 1 Corinthians 14:26,31; Ephesians 4:14-16.
18. Romans 12:3; Philippians 2:3.

Question for reflection

How well does the marathon picture work for the Church in terms of us all running together to improve our performance regardless of our previous race experience?

Chapter Three: Knockbacks Are Coming

You probably remember Weebles, those children's toys that have a rounded base with a weight in it, so no matter how hard you push, they'll always wobble back to where they started. Well, if only coping with life's knockbacks could be that easy; and initially I thought it would be. I had to learn the hard way that knockbacks can also be reality checks. Wobbling back instantly to our starting point is not always the best way to show that we have Christ's resurrection life within us.

For a long time I short-circuited the story of Paul's stoning in Lystra. When Luke wrote that they dragged him out of the city believing him to be dead, I knew that Luke would have been right. In those days they didn't stop pelting you until they were sure they'd killed you. As far as everyone was concerned, when they left Paul, he was only fit for burial. The fact that he recovered when the Christians gathered around him was a miracle, but in my mind I then had him striding off straight away to the next town to preach the gospel. In reality, he was taken to someone's home to recover, to have his bruises bathed and hopefully to get a decent night's sleep.[19] It was still a miracle, but a more realistic one. My first thought had been, 'Wow, he got up full of resurrection life, not a bruise on him; no time out to rest, no need to reflect, no need to recover. What an example!' But I was wrong.

Let me put it another way. I once heard someone say that when you listen to the way many of us preach, you could think that Jesus might just as well have come for a weekend rather than for thirty-plus years. I

---

19. Acts 14:1-20.

was in danger of going one step further and thinking 'a day could have done it'. Jesus could have risen on Friday evening.

Some of my simplistic thinking was reactionary. All my Christian life I've wanted to see people bounce back quickly. I would just love it if things could be this straightforward, and it pains me when they aren't. Even now it saddens me when new Christians have their enthusiasm dampened down by older believers wrongly implying that maturity and enthusiasm can't go hand-in-hand. But while I want to put in a big plea for believing in the bounce back, I do also want to speak up for the principle of allowing reality checks to work. Knockbacks shouldn't paralyse us, but I believe they should provoke us: not just to rise up in indignation but to rise up with greater wisdom.

After I'd had my summertime encounter with Jesus, I wanted the young people in the youth group to have an encounter with Jesus too. I knew of a Christian organisation that showed scientific films that ended with an evangelistic appeal, so I asked them to send one of their films. The person who brought it was a retired military officer. He introduced the film and watched from the back, but the forty teenagers were getting restless. They didn't really get on with the science. They were scraping their chairs and talking to each other. Suddenly the film was stopped and the young people were given a military-style dressing down: 'If you don't behave, you won't see the film!' To me that was a risky strategy. They would probably have welcomed him carrying out his threat. He retreated to the back of the hall and turned the film back on. After ten more minutes, the chairs were scraping again and the chatting had increased. The officer was back at the front warning them, just as if he were marshalling his troops. Then after a little more science, we arrived at the appeal. A person on-screen took his Bible off the shelf and began pointing out that, having seen the facts, it was time to respond in faith.

You could have heard a pin drop. It was just amazing. They all listened.

And then our military guest came to the front for a third time and said, 'Now, if you want to take that step of faith tonight you can give your life to Jesus. How many of you want to do that?' Thirty hands shot up, a 75 per cent response. 'No, no, no!' he said. 'Let's get this clear. You haven't understood me properly. How many of you really want to give your life to Jesus?' Again the same hands went up and they prayed a prayer of repentance and commitment with him.

I believed their commitment deserved endorsing, but the church members who were helping me run the group were sceptical and shrugged off the teenagers' responses, not wanting to provide any follow-up support for them. I felt the youth deserved better. To have such a knockback so early on seemed totally unfair. I began to wonder why I was studying dentistry and thought of preparing for church leadership by switching to theology. Being in an Anglican church I sent off an enquiry. This led to a knockback of my own. I was told, 'You are too young and too inexperienced. A degree in dentistry is as good as a degree in anything else. Finish the dentistry and apply again.' I'm sure all of this was true but I didn't take it well. My initial step into church leadership certainly hadn't gone as expected and, true to form, I wanted to bounce back.

Two opportunities to study theology had caught my eye and so I asked a medical student friend of mine to spend the summer praying with me about the possibility of my switching courses. When we started, he seemed totally set on completing his medical degree, but as we prayed, he felt he should give up medicine and go as a missionary to India. I was shocked. I thought I was the one who should be moving on, but I couldn't get away from some words in 1 Corinthians 7:20, 'Each person should remain in the situation they were in when God called them.' I can see now that I was taking them a bit out of context but I kept praying, 'God, is that really what you want me to do? You want me to stay and finish this course?' The answer was clear but the bounceback mechanism in me was strong and I was still restless. I had this idea that if you have been given resurrection life, nothing should hold you down. You've got to be out there, always busy, always doing something for God's kingdom. So, even though I went back to complete my degree, I also got the reading list from one of the theological colleges, thinking I would work my way through it in my spare time. In the end, trying to be the bounceback kid overloaded me and split my focus. I never finished the reading list.

During my clinical studies, I had read some other books, focusing on discipleship: Roy Hession's *Calvary Road*, George Verwer's *A Revolution of Love* and Margaret Cleator's *The God Who Answers by Fire*.[20] Gradually I began to realise that discipleship involves paying a price. Having resurrection life goes hand-in-hand with accepting the cross. My first reaction to this cross-embracing teaching was to say, 'Well, I've already done that. I accepted the cross when I said, "Jesus, you died in my place",[21] but then I started to see that it isn't just a once-for-all transaction. Paul told the church that he died 'daily' (1 Corinthians 15:31, NKJV). His secret of living the resurrection life was knowing how to embrace the knockbacks as well as the uplifts.

When we are looking at being built as living stones into God's unstoppable church,[22] it's pretty clear that humility helps. Unstoppable church isn't about pushing on regardless. It's about allowing the death of Christ to work in us so that the resurrection life of Christ can be seen.[23] Without these reality checks it's easy to become arrogant, seeing ourselves as invincible. Maybe, if at the time I'd reflected more on some of my early

20. Roy Hession, *The Calvary Road* (London: Christian Literature Crusade, 1950), George Verwer, *A Revolution of Love* (London: Pickering & Inglis Ltd., 1971), Margaret Cleator, *The God Who Answers by Fire* (London: Bible and Medical Missionary Fellowship, 1968).
21. Romans 5:8.
22. 1 Peter 2:5.
23. Philippians 3:10-11; Romans 8:11.

knockbacks, I would have made life easier for those around me; after all, I wasn't setting out to knock them back too.

But knowing *how* to fit in is one thing, knowing *where* to fit in is another. And it's something we can't be casual about. Fitting in involves commitment, and we need to be sure that we are in the right place if we're going to give it everything we've got. And being sure can take a lot of prayer, thoughtful reflection and faithful obedience to God's guidance. But the more we give, the more we'll gain.[24] That's the joy of commitment.[25]

Question for reflection

How can knockbacks contribute to our personal growth, and how important is humility when it comes to fitting into the Church?

---

24. Philippians 3:12.
25. James 1:2-3.

Chapter Four: A Time of Transition

I really like the contrast between Genesis 1 and Genesis 2. In Genesis 1 we have the overview of creation: God speaking and things happening. He says, 'Light' and there is light.[26] He says, 'Separate the waters' and that's exactly what happens.[27] But when we come into Genesis 2, we focus right down and are given a close-up of the place God is preparing for the man and woman he's going to pamper as representatives of the whole of humanity.[28] He wants them to have access to more of the life the man has already had breathed into him.[29] So, setting up everything appropriately is vital. This is detailed work. Instead of speaking, God is planting. Genesis 2:8 says: 'Now the LORD God had planted a garden in the east, in Eden'. I think this is amazing. It's a picture of God as a landscape artist: 'I'll put this here, and I'll put that there. This will be a river and here will be some trees' – full of attention right down to the tiniest flower. He knows exactly where each plant will grow best. And having created this haven, he puts Adam into it to care for it.

Now it's worth noticing that caring for it is all Adam has to do. He hasn't got to re-landscape it. He's not being told, 'Now you can change it all around and decide where to re-plant everything.' He is just being told to tend it.[30] And I wonder sometimes if we in our churches don't prefer to see ourselves as landscape artists rather than weeders and waterers. We just love digging ourselves up, checking out our roots

26. Genesis 1:3.
27. Genesis 1:6-7.
28. Genesis 2:8-9.
29. Genesis 2:7.
30. Genesis 2:15.

and replanting ourselves wherever we fancy. And if we see ourselves as leaders, we may become obsessed with doing this for others too. It would be far better to simply make sure that we are exactly where God wants us to be, doing exactly what God wants us to do. We need this kind of confidence in order to 'flourish' (Psalm 92:13).[31] We don't have to re-root every time the wind blows or weather conditions change. God is the landscape gardener. Knockbacks bring reality checks, but if relocation is being considered, it should be done by asking God and being ready to hear his answer.

For Paul, being in the right place at the right time, doing the right things was a vital part of his ministry. He wasn't only concerned about where he should be permanently based, but where he should be on a daily basis. As he travelled around, he wanted to know where he should visit, how long he should stay, what he should do and what he should say.[32] He was committed to preaching and pastoring, but if at times God told him to take up his old trade as a tentmaker to support his team and help make the most of his contacts, he was prepared to do it.[33] God was in control.

Now there came a point in Paul's travels when he took on a new apprentice, a young man called Timothy who was raised in Lystra, a place of mixed memories for Paul.[34] Once Timothy had been prayed for by his local church leaders, he moved on with Paul to break new ground.[35] As they travelled together, along with Silas, through what today is central and western Turkey, they tried to go into the Roman province of Asia in the west and then headed north towards the Black Sea. But Paul sensed no freedom from God to go into any of these

---

31. See also Psalm 1:3.
32. Acts 16:6-10.
33. Acts 18:3; 20:34-35.
34. Acts 14:19-20.
35. Acts 16:1-3.

places.[36] For Timothy, on his first missionary journey, nothing could have been clearer; being in the wrong place at the wrong time, trying to do the wrong thing with the wrong people, had no place in Paul's life and ministry. Having ended up at Troas on the Aegean coast, they just waited.[37]

Eventually, Paul had a vision in the night and saw a Macedonian pleading with him for help.[38] It was exactly what was needed, a clear call with a sense of purpose. This wasn't going to be a speculative journey, travelling by chance; or an ego trip, just seeking to add to an international tally. Here was a clear goal; a group of people needing their help.

When members of an unstoppable church have a personal confidence about place and purpose, it adds to the overall momentum. Without this confidence, neither they nor the church will grow. And how can we make sure that we are helping to generate this momentum in our church, and are able to make a difference where we are? We need to be bold enough to ask God, 'Where should I be going and what should I be doing?'

When I graduated as a dentist, I had to ask these questions. On one hand, there were job offers in London teaching hospitals and on the other, an assured route into church leadership through theological college. I prayed hard and thought hard, and for the second time in my life sensed that, from my growing knowledge of the Bible, a specific verse was pointing out the way. Again, it was not a verse I'd particularly sought out, and this time I was more mindful of its context. Irritatingly, it was just the first half of a verse – 'give back to Caesar what is Caesar's' (Matthew 22:21). My emotions would definitely have preferred the second half – '[give back] to God what is God's'. That would have been

---

36. Acts 16:4-7.
37. Acts 16:8.
38. Acts 16:9-10.

so much more exciting. The first half did make sense, though, as when I was a student our courses were covered by grants. I'd had a lot of education at government expense and needed to put something back. So, I took an appointment in a London teaching hospital.

I was certainly in the right place at the right time, but I started to feel restless and began looking for the next step, ideally a place where I could give back to God and Caesar at the same time. In the end I came up with a great idea. I could be a missionary, practising dentistry while planting churches. Strangely, an opportunity came up. A missionary dentist had died and his widow was keen to find someone to carry on his work. She had returned home and was staying near where I was living at the time. It all just seemed to fit together. I was so excited. I now knew what I was going to do with my life. And what was more, I'd recently met a certain nurse in the hospital where I was working, and knew who was going to be my wife. Incredibly, she was excited about my life plans too. Marion and I quickly lined everything up. The missionary society was keen to get us out as quickly as possible, and our local churches were committed to praying for us.

And then as suddenly as the opportunity arose, it disappeared.

The project we were to engage in ran into funding problems and we were put on hold. Once again, I found myself saying, 'God, where do you want me to be?' We didn't want to abandon our goal, but at the same time we found ourselves being drawn by the advice of a missionary who'd written, 'Don't try to do overseas what you haven't done at home.' So, difficult as it was, since we wanted to church-plant overseas, the question became, 'Where is there a church plant we can help with at home?' Well, the answer to that was simple, at least in my mind. I'd heard of a brand-new church plant in central Cornwall, and having grown to know Cornwall well, as I'd spent my university summers helping with children's work and preaching in churches there, we headed off for an exploratory weekend with me thinking, 'This is the place.' But it quickly became clear that I was wrong. I had, in my enthusiasm, run ahead without spending long enough listening to where God wanted me to go. But he's always working away behind the scenes, isn't he?

Somehow we arrived exactly where God wanted us to be, in south London, where Marion had felt all along she was meant to be studying midwifery. When she went for her interview at the maternity hospital, they said, 'We hear you're getting married. Would you like a house?' We were given a house for next to no rent and yet, still, something didn't feel quite right. I was sure I'd heard God say that we should serve overseas and church-plant. South London hardly seemed like a step on the way, but God is a far better re-locator than I could ever be and he was planting us where he could help us grow. I stopped trying to hold on to the mission field with one hand and God with the other, and decided to hold God with both hands, knowing that in holding him I was also holding our future.

We knew that Paul's commitment to being in the right place at the right time, saying and doing the right thing among the right people, had to be our commitment too.[39] We had also discovered that the only way to be sure of being in the right place was to seek God and go with his guidance.

There was, however, a complication. We had a physical house but no spiritual home, and my reflections on my student days were making me more and more convinced about the kind of church we should eventually be helping to plant. I had a growing sense that not only was the Church never intended to be divided into experts and learners, but it was never intended to be divided into followers and leaders either. Of course, we were all meant to be followers of Jesus, but somehow we were all meant to be leaders for Jesus too. I couldn't get it out of my

---

39. Acts 16:4-10.

mind that the whole discipleship programme that Jesus ran had this double goal of creating equality and stimulating progress.

Thoughts were shaping in my mind but I had no idea what a church full of would-be leaders could look like. Could south London offer such a possibility? I could see the elements of leadership development and equality within the Christian Union in my second year at university, but I wanted to explore more.

Question for reflection

As Christians, being in a place where we can grow is important, but God often plants us where we don't expect. How essential is it that we trust God for guidance, and how might our Bible knowledge help us in this?

Chapter Five: Follower to Leader

Andrew probably never thought that one day he'd be a leader. His married brother, Simon, always took the lead in the family.[40] And Simon was the leader in their business too. They ran a fishing boat together on Lake Galilee,[41] and Simon had been making his feelings known about Andrew following John the Baptist. 'What's the point of dreaming about a coming Messiah when there are catches to land?' But Andrew had decided how to put a stop to these challenges. He had just become one of the first to sign up as a follower of Jesus, and if he was following Jesus, then Simon had to follow Jesus too, even if it ran the risk of Simon trying to take charge of the little group around Jesus that was just beginning to gather. There was no easy way to persuade a man like Simon. The only thing to do was to introduce him to Jesus and let Jesus take control.[42]

Well, that encounter was just the beginning. Jesus summed up Simon in an instant when he called him Peter, the 'rock'.[43] And for the next three years Andrew watched his brother follow Jesus while being chiselled into a different kind of leader.[44] It was an interesting change – so absorbing that Andrew possibly never noticed how much of a leader he, the younger brother, was becoming at the same time. Jesus seemed determined to make sure that there would be no difference between those who were following him as leaders and those he was turning into

---

40. Matthew 8:14; Mark 1:29-30; Luke 4:38.
41. Matthew 4:18-19; Mark 1:16; Luke 5:1-3.
42. John 1:40-42.
43. Matthew 16:18.
44. Mark 5:37-42; Matthew 14:28-31; 17:1-8; 26:37; John 21:15-19.

leaders as they followed him. Everyone was being reshaped. Andrew was really good at bringing people to Jesus. He'd brought Simon at the start of Jesus' ministry, and then over the next few years made a pattern of it, often working with his friend Philip who'd brought Nathanael.[45] But this proved to be just the beginning. When the Holy Spirit came on the day of Pentecost, Andrew was empowered, along with 3,000 others[46] and took up his leadership role among the rest of the Eleven.[47] Like his brother, he'd become both a follower and a leader. Every follower *of* Jesus is designed to become a leader *for* Jesus.

There's a really interesting dynamic here. With Jesus we have leadership and togetherness working hand-in-hand. And the first thing we see is that if every follower is becoming a leader, it puts an end to the notion that some are born to lead and others are born to follow. We really are all expected to do both. A church where everyone can recognise everyone else's leadership role, and can give them space to get on and fulfil it at their own pace, will be an unstoppable church. The second thing we see is that the very leadership style itself that Jesus is shaping is fundamentally non-competitive. For a group to work well together when it is made up entirely of developing leaders, everyone has to accept at the very least that because they are a leader it doesn't mean they have to be leading the entire group.[48] We're talking about everyone becoming leaders in their own right and expressing that commitment enthusiastically in the church, in the home, in the workplace and in the community. It's the kind of leadership that focuses on a way of life and requires a consistent approach to living. The fitting together works because all who are leaders are still followers, looking to Jesus individually and together.

---

45. John 1:43-51.
46. Acts 1:12-13; 2:1-4; Acts 2:41.
47. Acts 2:14.
48. Matthew 20:20-28; Mark 10:35-45.

I might not have realised any of this if I hadn't been given a great discipleship template. It speaks to leaders who are still prepared to be followers, and came when I was least expecting it.

During the year I was working in London teaching hospitals, with Zambia in view, I spoke to a Baptist minister friend of mine about believers' baptism. He kindly arranged for me to be baptised as part of a Sunday evening service in his church. Having never attended such a service, I had no idea that Baptist ministers like to select a Bible verse for each person being baptised. So I didn't see how significant it was when I arrived for the service to have my friend admit to me that he hadn't been able to find a verse. I just shrugged it off, thinking it was probably because we'd been close for some years and he knew me too well. Anyway, I had more practical things on my mind, such as how do you actually baptise someone by immersion, and when in the service does it take place? He gave me some simple directions: 'Hold my wrist, keep your legs straight and you'll be fine!', adding that I'd be baptised after he'd preached the sermon. I found somewhere to sit, put my towel under the chair and waited for the start of the service. Apparently, I was the only one being baptised.

The service was moving along nicely. We'd sung and we'd prayed and I was invited to say why I believed I should be baptised. My friend then went to the pulpit to read out the text for his sermon. Before he began, he told everyone he hadn't been able to settle on a verse for me but went on to say he'd chosen a whole Bible passage. It was Revelation 3:7-13, Christ's letter to the church at Philadelphia. I tried to listen intently as he read it, but was relieved when he said, 'I'll explain it line by line.'

The first part caught my attention. It was all about open doors – 'I have placed before you an open door that no one can shut' (v. 8). It was a great promise, but it made me rather uncomfortable, as the leadership style I'd honed at school and university had specialised in pushing hard on closed and stubborn doors until I got my way. My friend must have known this about me, as I'd often opened up to him in the midst of my frustrations. I sensed, though, that he was correcting me graciously, just letting the Bible do its work. The verse went on: 'I know that you have little strength, yet you have kept my word and have not denied my name.' It seemed that, as far as God was concerned, doors weren't to be opened by a forceful foot but by us acknowledging our limitations, putting God's Word into practice, and being faithful to Jesus in all things.

Wow. That was just step one of the sermon and I was already having to do some rethinking. Keeping God's Word, being faithful? They seemed fine! Acknowledging my limitations? Mmm...

We moved on to difficult relationships. The church in Philadelphia obviously had problems with a satanic cult, which I guess must be the ultimate in opposition, guaranteed to overwhelm anyone. The answer to their predicament, though, wasn't an indignant calling down of judgement from heaven, but the promise of a total turn-around that would see the cult's hateful resistance give way to respectful submission. As I wasn't facing any hateful opposition at the time, I was tempted to tuck this one away for future reference, but I was struck by the fact that the cult members' turn-around hinged on their recognition of God's love for the Philadelphian believers. I wondered if there might ever be a time when people would turn around because they could see how much God loved me; a kind of 'if-God's-love-can-change-him-then-God-must-be-amazing' moment. It sounded impossible and the most unlikely way of winning people over that had ever been invented, but these were the verses my friend had chosen for me so I had to sit up and take notice.

We got to point three: 'Since you have kept my command to endure patiently, I will also keep you from the hour of trial that is going to come on the whole world' (v. 10). I had no idea what the hour of trial might be, but I spotted that protection was linked to patient endurance.

Again, this was totally back-to-front to my way of thinking. Apparently, protection can come as a gift to those who patiently put up with things, rather than something that has to be fought for. Unbelievable! So far it had been a sermon full of surprises, a message delivered by a friend who'd been praying hard for me. Whether he realised it or not, his words were hitting home: accepting limitations, being loved and showing patience. I had no idea what else could lie in store.

When we got to verse 12, I glimpsed a picture of an eternal reward, the prize of becoming an immovable pillar, strong and stable, set in God's temple and sealed with the names of the Father, the new Jerusalem, and Jesus, the Son of glory and love. It went into my thinking ready to emerge much later at a crucial point in my life and leadership and, for us, in a later chapter of this book. Limitations, love and patience were still at the front of my mind.

For Baptists, believers' baptism is a symbolic re-enactment. It marks the personal 'death and resurrection' transformation that happens when someone makes a considered response in repentance and faith to the good news that there's new life for us in Christ Jesus. Going down into the water signifies the burial of the past and coming up out of the water signifies rising to new life.[49] I hadn't expected the evening to have worked out as it had, but as we went into the water and my friend stood alongside me ready to plunge me backwards and (hopefully) haul me up again, I sensed that I was entering something new in terms of my life and my leadership.

It may sound as if what my friend presented to me from Revelation 3 was more about lifestyle than about leadership, and I know that there are schools of thought that think that it's possible to live one way and lead another, but I don't believe that's what God is looking for. The characteristics we need as followers *of* Jesus are the ones that we need

---

49. Romans 6:4; Colossians 2:12.

as leaders *for* Jesus; acknowledging that we have little strength, are loved by Jesus and are willing to patiently press on. Kicking down doors, demanding submission and fighting for self-protection are not the way God wants us to be. Good leaders bring people with them rather than alienate people from them.

There's a famous fable about the wind and the sun arguing over who's stronger. Eventually they see a man walking along a road and decide to set up a contest based on removing his coat. The wind goes first and begins by blowing gently. The coat starts to flap. Encouraged by this early success, the wind blows harder. The coat is now flapping wildly. Convinced success is now in sight, the wind gives one more massive blow, only to see the man wrap his coat around himself even more tightly. The sun laughs and tells the wind to step aside. Shining effortlessly out of a now calm sky, it only takes a few minutes for the sun's heat to persuade the man to take off his coat.[50] Warmth and graciousness are great ways of getting cooperation, and getting cooperation is what good leadership is all about.

This is the kind of leadership that God wants to take us all into, and we need to remember that in Philadelphia, as with the disciples around Jesus, they were developing this leadership lifestyle together. If there is one thing that could make all our churches unstoppable, it would be for us to find a way of encouraging every follower of Jesus to work with others as leaders for Jesus along the lines of Revelation 3:7-13.

Right now, God is looking at you. He sees you as a leader and he wants you to grasp hold of this with both hands. As you keep following him, he is discipling you to take a lead in his kingdom – in your home, in your workplace and in your community. And he wants you to be contributing powerfully in his Church, not just as a pew-warmer but

50. www.online-literature.com/aesop/aesops-fables/60/ (accessed 18.12.23).

as an inspirer and encourager of others.[51] You have more in you than you realise and he is determined that the brightness of the light he has put in you, and the dynamism of the life he has given you, will be seen. You are a living stone, an essential part of his unstoppable church.

Question for reflection

Jesus made sure that he developed his twelve closest disciples, whom he was preparing to train the Church, to be leaders as well as followers. How did they pass on lessons of leadership development in their teaching?

---

51. Hebrews 10:25.

Chapter Six: An Early Spring

We have come a long way in our first five chapters. We've talked about togetherness and highlighted the importance of knowing *where* God wants us to fit. We've now talked about leadership, and seen the kind of person God wants us to be in order to fit. So the question is – what *kind* of commitment will we need to make to see this togetherness and leadership development working out in practice?

Well, I guess we all have those moments when we wish that the sun would always shine, and there are parts of the world that don't have seasons. But if we are going to be serious about commitment, we'll quickly discover that even if we were to live where the climate never changes, we'd still be facing ups and downs and going through seasons in our lives. And keeping seasons in mind can be good. We are, after all, thinking about committing in a way that will help to recapture the momentum of the early Church, and that's the passion that led to our various denominations and churches being birthed too. It's a big commitment, and if at any point it starts to get tough, we can always remind ourselves that spring is round the corner.

But we are going to start with a positive story. We've already seen that Paul, the travelling church-planter, was always facing new assignments in new areas with new relationships. It was the nature of his job. Often the reactions he got must have made him feel that sunny acceptance could give way to wintery rejection in a blink of an eye.[52] Generally, though, he knew that when a visit was cut short, he'd be back at some point for a

---

52. Acts 14:8-19.

longer stay.[53] But there was one city where he did stay longer, benefiting from the warmth of acceptance for an extended eighteen-month period. That was Corinth.[54] And somewhat unusually for Paul, the longer he stayed the easier it seemed to become. So let's look at Corinth and see the three factors that may well have lengthened his stay. Hopefully they can also act as markers on our own journey of commitment.

Now, being Paul, when he arrived in Corinth he'd already checked out that, as far as God was concerned, he was in the right place, at the right time, ready to say and do the right things with the right people. But experience had already taught him that there was no guarantee that this was going to make it easy for him. Before he reached Corinth he'd been in Philippi where he'd discovered that finding welcoming friendships can help. In Philippi, Lydia hadn't only opened her heart to God but had opened her home to Paul and his team.[55] On arriving in Corinth he was equally blessed by coming across Aquila and Priscilla. They were a couple who'd recently moved to Corinth when Emperor Claudius had expelled all Jewish residents from Rome. They ran a tentmaking business from their home, probably as part of a supply chain for the Roman army and, as Paul had once made tents for a living, he moved in with them and worked alongside them. It gave the three of them a great opportunity to bond together in friendship. Aquila and Priscilla thought it was great, as they were learning to lead alongside Paul.

By the time Silas and Timothy arrived in Corinth from Macedonia, Paul was already well settled, working with Aquila and Priscilla and speaking in the synagogue. Their arrival prompted him to be more outspoken, which really upset the synagogue congregation. But Paul himself was unperturbed and simply set up a meeting in the house next door. Remarkably,

---

53. Acts 17:1-10 and Acts 20:1-2.
54. Acts 18:1-18.
55. Acts 16:14-15.

despite the move, the ruler of the synagogue then came to believe in Jesus, along with his whole family. This had a big impact on all sorts of people, and meant that Paul's ministry in Corinth was now expanding. It's not difficult to imagine that, given the friendship and growing success, Paul could well have been hovering on the brink of a longer-term commitment. So when the Lord spoke to him at night, assuring him that there were a lot more people in the city who would believe, it must have come as confirmation.[56] On top of that, God promised Paul that he wouldn't have to face any attack or hurt in Corinth, which must have been great news, but personal safety was never a priority on Paul's list of terms and conditions. With this promise in mind, he must have been quite bemused when well into his time in the city, a group from the Jewish community dragged him before Gallio, the Roman proconsul.[57] It may have just seemed par for the course and the promise might not even have crossed his mind, but before he could open his mouth, Gallio dismissed the case.[58] Admittedly the incident then sparked some tension between the Jewish and Greek communities in the city, but Gallio's continuing calmness made sure it didn't get out of hand. Paul, of course, remained unhurt.[59]

Now I think it's fair to say that friendship, fruitfulness and divine confirmation could give our assurance and confidence a boost as we seek to commit more fully to where God has placed us. But as I'm sure we're all aware, constant sunshine isn't always going to be our experience as we work through our commitment. Corinth was a great experience for Paul, but he would be the first to understand it if our journey of commitment turns out to have some chillier moments between the positives of friendship, fruitfulness and divine confirmation.

When we arrived in south London we had a home, Marion had

---

56. Acts 18:9-11.
57. Acts 18:11-13.
58. Acts 18:14-16.
59. Acts 18:17.

a training course, and I quickly tracked down a vacancy in a dental practice. What we didn't have was a church where we could learn about church-planting. A friend of a friend pointed us to a meeting in someone's home. I arrived one Sunday morning when Marion was working a weekend shift and, despite all of our missionary training about embedding in the culture, I struggled. A few family members and friends in a living room was not what I'd been expecting. It all felt overly informal, even more informal than the Christian Union meetings from my early student days and, to be honest, it seemed more than a little bit… well, if I'm to think of a word, perhaps 'obscure'. I remember thinking, 'How ever is God going to find us here?' This was totally inappropriate of me and clearly one of my early mistakes, but we stayed, journeying with the host couple as they went through two house moves. Within two years, now married with a son and a second child on the way, we found ourselves buying the house opposite their latest rented property. Believe it or not, this was when we really began to discover what commitment could be about. From the moment we moved in, everyone thought of our home as 'church house number two'.

I don't know if you can imagine the arrangement, but it had a kind of communal living feel to it. It was a case of 'No one claimed that any of their possessions was their own' (Acts 4:32). We had two pluses a house guest who was keen to decorate, and a really well-stocked garden that I was eager to enjoy, not least because it was well-planted with great groundcover to reduce the maintenance. One day when I was at work, our house guest, in consultation with our neighbour across the road, decided that the garden would be better stripped bare. I came home to find myself standing, disbelieving, at the bottom of my barely recognisable garden while trying to come to terms with the realisation that I had also landed at the bottom of an equally daunting learning curve – a curve which was just about to get a whole lot steeper.

As the church grew in the house opposite, I was given occasional opportunities to teach. I'd also been introducing a number of students from the college Christian Unions where I'd been speaking. All in all, I thought that over the two years I'd settled in pretty well. But someone had spotted that despite the missionary society's best endeavours at teaching us that working cross-culturally was about embedding rather than living in two worlds, I still had a bit of a 'them and us' mindset. At times I still saw myself as an apprentice church-planter, and perhaps increasingly as a budding travelling speaker, rather than just one of the group. It was time for me to be challenged. I was invited across the road and rang the doorbell with some trepidation. We sat in the lounge, just two of us. It felt strange. The room was normally packed and I was generally assigned to the piano stool. Then the list began; all the things I had been getting wrong, described one after another as 'and here's another nail in your coffin'. My teaching opportunities were put on hold for three months.

On reflection, without this one-to-one conversation I wouldn't have had a clue about my shortcomings. Funnily enough, it occurred to me at the time that a three-month ban from the piano stool could have been equally challenging and helpful to me. When everyone else was sitting on dining chairs, in armchairs or on a sofa, I was at least three inches higher, and that was not a good idea in a meeting where everyone's opportunity to participate equally was highly prized. I had clearly been more prominent than I should have been. I walked back across the road with a lot to reflect on. In a session that had lasted less than an hour, I'd been given an understanding of Christian ministry that I knew I'd never forget. I'd seen myself as a teacher but had now been challenged to get myself better equipped. I knew from the Bible, as I guess we all do, that God has provided apostles, prophets, evangelists and pastors, as well as teachers,[60] but I hadn't realised just how much I needed to be strengthened in my areas of weakness. The three-month embargo was especially designed to give me a chance to think through how I might develop as a pastor. But I had no idea what to do, other than to pray and trust that God would work a miracle. The period coincided with the last three months of Marion's pregnancy.

I had obviously hit a winter season in my journey of commitment. But before we all start piling on our protective layers in sympathy, let's move on quickly to my positive outcome, my early spring. And it literally was an early spring that made all the difference.

It was mid-February, and our daughter was a few days old. A member of the church had called in to help me with some ironing. While I was clearing up our son's toys around her, she started saying, 'I don't know what happened to you a couple of months back, but I suddenly felt I could talk to you about anything.' I could hardly believe it. Despite all of my hoping and praying, I hadn't gone through any sudden transformative moment. But things must have been going on under the surface. I smiled as I thought of something Marion and I had noticed the day our daughter was born. As I continued to clear the toys, I deliberately glanced out of the window, now fully aware that our previously bare garden, which had lost all its groundcover, had become full of crocuses and daffodils. All along, unbeknown to me, bulbs were hidden under the grass.

And there's a further sequel, which coincidentally showed me how quickly things can move on in a church that has few formal structures. It took me completely by surprise. Not only had someone gone to the trouble of sitting me down and giving me a crash course on improving my leadership skills, but they'd obviously been looking out for an opportunity for me to put them into practice. A few months after my embargo

---

60. Ephesians 4:11.

ended, I was made an elder. The owners of the rented house opposite had decided to sell, and the house some distance away that the couple hosting the church had chosen to buy was in need of serious refurbishment. The church was going to need a temporary home. Another young dad had been made an elder at the same time as me, and it was decided that half the church should go to his home (and that would include the students I'd brought) and half to mine. My first real experience of church leadership was to be as a substitute pastor of half a church in our home on short-term loan. I was definitely fully committed. I now had to be ready for the next phase, which meant putting these newly acquired pastoral skills into practice.

I'm mindful, though, that I could be giving the impression that church leadership has to be the focus of everyone's commitment. To be honest, since joining a church in which equality worked, it had ceased to be my goal. I'd become happy just being part, putting my all into the dental practice, and serving wherever required – even from the piano stool. But now as we go forward, I can give a little more insight into togetherness and leadership from a church leader's perspective.

Question for reflection

Despite our best intentions it is possible to hold on to a 'them and us' way of thinking. This has to go if belonging to a local church is to be the transformative, relational experience that God intends. How important for you is your commitment to your local church?

Chapter Seven: The Green Cloth

When we agreed to take the rented house that Marion was offered at her midwifery interview, we'd very little idea of what lay behind the generosity. Once we'd moved in, it was obvious that the house had no personal markers at all: no books, no pictures, no photographs, no little ornaments; nothing to suggest it wasn't just a house bought to furnish and let. But houses like that don't have a piano, or feel quite so much like a family home. Tragically, our landlady had lost her husband and son in a road accident. There was an open plywood box in the spare bedroom that we were told held the landlady's possessions. It had a few small furniture items on the top of it. One day we were asked to repack the box ready for a house move.

We began by carefully moving the loose items that we thought might get damaged in the removal van, and began wrapping them carefully and setting them aside ready for repacking. As we did this, we caught sight of a green cloth. By the time we were halfway down the box, there it was, spread right across with a handwritten note fixed to it with a safety pin. The sign said: 'Don't go beyond this unless you're sure'. We knew the instruction was for our landlady rather than for us, but we still lifted the corner cautiously. There were the missing personal items: the books, the pictures, the photographs, the little ornaments; all the evidence of her personal life. It was an awkward moment. Deciding to go no further, we gently replaced the cloth. We felt the intensity of her pain. We looked at each other and understood why her healing might take some time.

Those few moments in the spare room with the plywood box taught us a lesson about pastoral care we'll never forget. A lot of people have 'green cloths' hiding areas of their lives which they're struggling to face up to. They should only be lifted with care in a setting where people are able to handle the issues. We'd all like to think our churches are great at doing this, but people who've been wounded by life's tragedies are not always so sure. They can find our sympathy fussy and pressurising when they know that time and distance could actually be more helpful. Sadly, church members are often the last to read the label: 'Don't go beyond this unless you're sure'.

This should all be prompting us to think about pastoral care in a church where the focus is on developing every member's leadership potential. If the church gets this right, it shouldn't be wholly dependent on putting on special pastoral care courses. An emphasis on 'whole church' discipleship, where everyone interacts with each other – learning, praying and worshipping together – should create the momentum needed to spur everyone to greater maturity. But getting it right is important, both for those who are already with us and for those who will be joining us. Accepting everyone unconditionally takes leadership qualities, and those qualities grow as our non-judgemental, unconditional acceptance is tested over time. If leadership development for all is our goal, then seeing leadership potential in everyone and accepting them accordingly has to be in everybody's mind from the outset.

A lot of Paul's evangelistic campaigns have been summarised for us by Luke in the book of Acts, but at least one must have happened after the last page. Paul's ship had toyed with harbouring in Crete as he had sailed as a prisoner to Rome,[61] and we can tell from his letter to Titus that at some point following his release from house arrest, he must have returned to Crete to preach across the length and breadth of the island. He had then left Titus to stay on to establish churches.[62]

---

61. Acts 27:12-13.
62. Titus 1:5.

We know that Paul could be very pastoral. Writing to the church in Thessalonica he said that he was gentle among them as 'a nursing mother cares for her children' (1 Thessalonians 2:7). But more often than not, Paul's pastoral care involved challenging whole churches, often by letter, and expecting them to address issues together as they responded jointly to his teaching. It's a strategy we seem to have lost sight of in our overly individualised world. It does, however, fit well with an understanding of a church where everybody is learning to lead together. As an approach it may lack sentimental appeal, but that's because we all too often prefer to swap the picture of the workmanlike shepherd caring for the flock for one of a dewy-eyed, smiling shepherd with a single sheep wrapped lovingly around their neck.

Do we really think that in Jesus's story, the shepherd left the ninety-nine every day to look for a different sheep that had wandered off?[63] If so, he would have needed sheep that could really watch out for themselves and each other. Interestingly, I do think having a watchful flock has a part to play in establishing good pastoral care in a church where every follower of Jesus is becoming a leader for Jesus, but it needs to be a mature watchfulness. All too often pastoral care is left solely to the church leader, and it's fairly obvious that wayward sheep will be less likely to wander away from a flock where all watch out for each other. Throughout his ministry, Jesus clearly expected a growing level of pastoral leadership from those around him,[64] the kind of maturity that even in a tightly knit group respects the importance of timing and distance regarding each other's problems.[65]

I'm sure we can all think of occasions in the Gospels when Jesus pinpointed individuals' shortcomings, but he generally did it far less

---

63. Luke 15:3-6.
64. Luke 9:1-6.
65. Galatians 6:2.

publicly than we may have imagined.[66] Just because millions of us have read the accounts since, doesn't mean that people's problems were paraded before millions at the time. Jesus rarely said all that he knew, and hardly ever drew attention to more than one thing at a time that needed correcting.[67] He was so pastorally aware that he didn't even switch off this awareness when he was relaxing with his friends. It must have been unbelievably hard for him during his final Passover meal to mention that one of the Twelve would betray him.[68] What was even more amazing, though, was that after three years of travelling together, the Eleven had no idea that Jesus was talking about Judas. They didn't even know that their treasurer had been helping himself to the funds.[69] In shepherding them, Jesus was far more interested in encouraging them to go forward together to find fresh pasture than to have them all penned up and bleating over each other's problems. He never gave them the opportunity to pick on Judas. For three years he knew what he knew and kept it to himself.

So back to Paul and Titus. Paul was totally committed to seeing people going on together and could be quite pointed when he wrote to churches about obstacles he saw blocking people's growth.[70] He didn't spare those who were keen to return to a slavish keeping of the law, and was equally blunt with those who were easy about going back to their old patterns of sinful behaviour.[71] When it came to the people of Crete, he made it crystal clear to Titus that laziness and gossiping posed a real threat to raising churches on the island.[72] Of course, I don't actually know how lazy and gossipy the people of Crete were in Paul's

66. Luke 9:54-55.
67. Mark 10:21; Luke 10:41-42.
68. See for example Matthew 26:21.
69. John 12:6.
70. Galatians 5:7.
71. Galatians 3:1-5; 4:8-11.
72. Titus 1:5-16.

day, but I know that people who are lazy, despite never making claims to leadership, can set a pattern that others quickly follow, and within weeks everyone's shortcomings are known to all and are being openly discussed everywhere. What's really bad is that gossiping undermines the hope of people having their issues resolved over time as they respond to sound teaching. It's hard for anyone to thrive in such a negative and discouraging atmosphere. Titus had a battle on his hands.

My task was nowhere near as challenging. Initially I was simply caring for a group of people who'd grown together over several years, with many already seeing themselves as leaders. But they were people on loan, and in less than a year, when the work on the original host's new home was complete, many of them left to meet there. Marion and I were willing to go too, but were encouraged to stay put and start building again. But as we did so, God seemed to be sending us living stones that needed help to get growing. In all probability they were no different from anyone who'd joined us before, but now I had pastoral responsibility, I was more likely to see the problems. I certainly wasn't rushing to rip away whatever people were using to hide their hurts and hindrances, but I do remember asking God, as I looked around the room one day, 'What happens if all these problems come to the surface at once?' I heard him say, as plainly as anything, 'They won't.' I immediately replied, 'How do you know?' I then spent the rest of the meeting trying not to laugh at my stupidity while marvelling at God's very practical way of dealing with things. I could see that our pastoral care course was not going to be something I had to design and insert into our timetable, but a hands-on training programme scheduled by God.

In readiness I had to set out some ground rules. It was clear that we weren't going to get anywhere if we tried to categorise people according to what we thought might be the depth of their problems. We needed to give everyone equal space to grow, and we were definitely not going to divide ourselves into 'those who'd arrived *to help*' and 'those who'd come *to be helped*'. In truth, most of us were in both camps. Recognising that could be our first step to maturity, and developing a sense of responsibility for covering each other's backs and speaking well of each other could be our second.

Given that we were all keen to grow, it was great that God was bringing together such a mixed group. A young man who as a sixth-former had visited us a lot in the early days of our marriage returned from university to base himself with us. Another young man who'd been caught up in a local branch of an international cult came to live in our home as he readjusted. A drug rehabilitation project closed down and some of the residents headed in our direction too. And all of those who joined us were quick to introduce their friends and contacts.

A particularly surprising introduction came from a nurse who'd recently linked up with us. She was working on a ward when a new student nurse collapsed. It turned out that the student had given birth over the weekend and had put her baby into foster care some distance away. The first thing we had to do was to collect the baby and reunite her with her mum. But we soon discovered that this particular student nurse had only just arrived from Zambia and that she'd grown up on the exact rural compound with its schools and clinic that we'd been assigned to. It was a strange fulfilment of a word of encouragement that someone had given us when our missionary plans were falling through a year or so before, 'Maybe God doesn't want you to go to Africa; maybe he'll send Africa to you.'

We were now having our first experience of Africa, and it was in our home; at first, just through a baby, but later with both mother and child. Our busy home was a joy for the three children – our two and the daughter of our latest house guest – as well as for the three of us as adults, and the church. Our house guest was very mischievous and loved pushing the cultural boundaries in our quiet south London suburb. She would visit the shops as if she were still in rural Zambia, with our daughter, instead of hers, tied onto her back by a wrap. She loved the bizarreness of such cultural clashes, and the cheerfulness with which she handled them made the real issue of learning to live in each other's shoes much easier. Lots of laughs can save a lot of tears and strengthen everyone's commitment to wholeheartedly accepting one another. This young wife and mother (we were later to meet the husband) was as well-versed in city life as she was in rural living. Her endless sense of fun and sharp-eyed perceptiveness played a huge part in setting the right atmosphere in the church. Churches with a strong sense of purpose can easily become rather intense and claustrophobic – we were spared that, and discovered an enjoyable lightness and fun-filled freedom that we were determined never to lose.

These very varied early additions, and there were many of them, meant a lot to us. The diversity was great, a real cross-section of ages and backgrounds. Our numbers were not far short of those in some churches around us that were blessed with buildings, and yet the sense of togetherness was holding firm. We believed that every person God sent had amazing potential, and our greatest joy was in noticing how everyone recognised that potential in each other. For me, it seemed that if we kept going in the same direction, we might gain a real sense of what pastoral care looked like in a church where every follower of Jesus was becoming a leader for Jesus. At the same time, though, it was clear that if we forgot that we were still a work in progress, our immaturity could push us either into making our new arrivals feel overwhelmed or leaving them feeling undervalued. We had to read people rightly by respecting their individuality. It wasn't lost on us that when Paul wrote to the Thessalonian church, 'Now about your love for one another we do not need to write to you, for you yourselves have been taught by God' (1 Thessalonians 4:9), it was undoubtedly a tribute to a lot of growing up over a long period of time, probably with more than a few slip-ups along the way.

But I don't want to set up too glossy a picture. In a church where everyone is equally accepted, there'll be times when some would like to be accepted a little more than others. Where the overall expectation is that everyone's problems will be solved along the way as we come together to learn, pray, have fellowship and break bread, there will be those who believe their issues deserve more attention, and sometimes they may be right. The challenge this creates is how to meet the needs of the few without taking away from the momentum of the whole, especially as that momentum is benefiting the few as much as everyone else. There seemed to be no easy answer. We certainly didn't want a twin-track church, so it was vital to find a way of keeping everyone going forward together.

There was a popular saying at the time that summed up an approach we'd been working hard to avoid: 'God brings people together to knock the corners of each other'.[73] The apparent rough and tumble of this may have appealed to some among us, but to most of us it seemed to be a very haphazard approach to pastoral care and lacked respect for people's potential. The picture it came from was great: stones in a riverbed becoming smooth as they were being moved along together by the flowing of the water. But without the flowing of the water, you have a disaster. I once asked a public health inspector of a new town development built with concrete blocks, what he had to inspect in such an obviously sterile environment. 'Rats,' he said. 'We've got endless rat runs from where the builders knocked the corners of the blocks.' That settled it. I had no desire to lead a church full of rat runs. I needed a new metaphor; knocking off the corners was not for me.

---

73. Source unknown.

The first idea that came into my head was that those wanting more attention were like pupils needing extra tutorials to keep up. As a model it had its appeal, admittedly more from the Old Testament than the New. But I did like the fact that back in Nehemiah's day when Ezra read from the Law in the open square, there were Levites scattered among the crowd to help people understand what was being read to them.[74] My hope was that our one-to-one sessions could be done more privately without drawing attention to those needing help. After all, we were all working on putting what we were learning into practice in our daily lives. In time, though, I felt challenged as some of those I was seeking to help more specifically seemed to feel they were carrying so much baggage that the gap between being a hearer of the Word and a doer would always remain too large for them to close.[75] This made me wish I could blast their negativity away with some high-powered spiritual dynamite, but I was aware there had been a rule when building Solomon's Temple that there was to be no sound of a hammer or chisel within the Temple precincts. Hammers and chisels belonged in the quarry, and in more recent times dynamite belongs there too.[76]

All of us were repeatedly facing the need for lifestyle adjustments and were content to spend time in God's presence alone to have these adjustments made. It was a good way of ensuring that we fitted together well. In the end I went with the Temple-building metaphor and began to see my one-to-one times with those who were struggling as my opportunity to get them on the cart to go back to the quarry for some real one-to-one reshaping by God. It was an obscure metaphor that defined the problem well, but it didn't make it any easier to resolve. I began to see that for us all to keep on growing together, we'd need to

---

74. Nehemiah 8:7-9.
75. James 1:22.
76. 1 Kings 6:7.

create some additional inspiration and space for those who were slower to fulfil their potential. Everyone was doing a great job at encouraging one another, but we needed a few exceptional inspirers and space creators to act as role models and to keep the whole atmosphere light and open without losing its challenge.

It was reassuring to see that Paul had advised Titus to adopt the same approach in Crete. When he'd challenged the laziness and gossiping, he was to 'appoint elders' in every city (Titus 1:5).

Question for reflection

How necessary is it for a church to ensure that confidentiality is maintained in a context of widespread encouragement, and how can this be done well?

Chapter Eight: Of Pillars and Porches

I love the story of Sir Christopher Wren and the Guildhall at Windsor. Wren, a British architect who back in the seventeenth century designed London's St Paul's Cathedral, was a brilliant mathematician, and allegedly he designed the Guildhall to be supported on relatively few pillars, prompting the city officials to say that he should have allowed for more. Visitors to the Guildhall can look up and see that the additional pillars stop short of the ceiling. They stand there to this day carrying no weight at all.

The apostle Paul had a thing about pillars. After some years of working on his own in his home area of Cilicia, Barnabas had brought him to Antioch. It was an interesting challenge for Paul (Saul as he was then) to settle once again into a church with a team leadership. So, when the opportunity came for him and Barnabas to visit Jerusalem, he was keen to go and take a closer look at how things operated there. Titus, a young Gentile Christian, was with them.[77]

The last time Paul had been in Jerusalem he had briefly met Peter, and James, the brother of Jesus.[78] When they arrived this time, Herod had just killed James, the brother of John, and was holding Peter in prison.[79] Miraculously, Peter was released and before Paul and Barnabas left for Antioch, Paul was able to see how Peter, John and James, the half-brother of Jesus who was picking up responsibility from his recently executed namesake, were able to work together. For Paul, they were the

77. Galatians 2:3-5.
78. Galatians 1:18-19.
79. Acts 12:1-5.

pillars of the Jerusalem church, making room for everyone else in the church to function.[80]

It is really important that, when we think about role models, we endorse the right people. There are so many factors to take into account that we can easily make a wrong choice. If we, like Paul, think in terms of pillars, we need to make sure we appoint people who are strong, stable and generous-spirited enough to make space for others. There's no sense in selecting people who can't carry the weight or are unstable. That will be a recipe for church collapse. But equally, if we appoint small-minded people they will act as short pillars, constricting the church and stunting people's growth.

We'd had a great beginning as a church and needed more physical space. As the church was in our home, it had seemed sensible quite early on to move to a larger house. But we had quickly filled that and began to look at renting a community hall. It wasn't just physical space we needed, though. Jesus had been amazing with the Twelve, avoiding intensity among his followers by constantly bringing friendship and perspective into the group and maintaining a lightness of spirit. We needed people like our young Zambian mum – who'd moved with her daughter to be with her husband in Canada – as she'd been great at doing just that. But there were other considerations too. Our approach to pastoral care was giving us plenty of scope for peer mentoring, but the idea of having some extra reference points, particularly for those needing additional input, definitely appealed. Paul's strategy of appointing elders in every city came to mind, and that brought us back to his letter to Titus. He'd written out a checklist for eldership appointments in Crete.[81]

When we look at this list today, we have to remember that Titus

---

80. Acts 12:6-18; Galatians 2:6-10.
81. Titus 1:6-9; see also 1 Timothy 3:2-7.

had more than the list to go on. He knew exactly what Paul was trying to achieve. He'd been with him on his visit to Jerusalem and almost certainly had seen for himself on Paul's third missionary journey the kind of people Paul had previously appointed in Derbe, Lystra, Iconium and Pisidian Antioch. He may well also have had a brief meeting with Aquila and Priscilla in Ephesus before Paul sent him on to Corinth.[82] In addition he'd seen how the team worked in his home church at Antioch.[83] Having clear examples in mind always helps.

As I looked at the list in south London nearly 2,000 years later, I summarised: good person, family minded,[84] servant-hearted, unselfish, calm, not given to drink, not greedy, committed to hospitality, appreciative, fair-minded, clear-thinking, clean living, having a good grasp of God's Word and an ability to explain what they'd learned to others. It was an amazing list and all the more so given that when Paul first started applying these principles in Galatia he was having to select from relatively new Christians, relying on their experience in life as well as their experience in Christ. Titus faced the same challenge in Crete, but we seemed to be in a better place as God had been adding to us people of my parents' age, plus a few who'd retired, and some of these had years of experience in Christ as well as in life.

Some newly emerging churches were making much of the parenting model, with lead couples choosing to be known as Mum and Dad. That never sat comfortably with me, but one older couple had caught my eye, and I was wondering whether to go with their parental approach. Given this, I was surprised when I was told that the husband had leadership

---

82. 2 Corinthians 2:13; 7:13-16.
83. Acts 13:1.
84. I love the fact that Paul, as a single person with single people in leadership roles around him, appreciated and encouraged the family nature of church. It is something that many single people not only greatly value but about which they are often particularly insightful.

aspirations he hoped to fulfil through me. Although I never mentioned these comments to anyone, I was beginning to see that the leadership style I was cultivating did leave me vulnerable to takeover bids from people who expected a more assertive approach. Even so, I had no idea that a full-blown challenge was just around the corner. It's very tempting when writing like this to leave out my mistakes, but I did learn a lesson that is worth passing on.

I had been chatting with one of the young men about his interest in a young woman who had recently joined us. I wanted to make sure he wasn't simply being swept along by the spate of other relationships that had been forming in what was still predominantly a youthful church. I talked to him as a friend but his body language may have given the hint that I'd left him feeling somewhat discouraged. Surprisingly, the older person I was thinking of bringing alongside me stepped in and confronted me about my advice to the couple. Apart from thinking it was a strange issue over which to be challenged, especially as I had no intention of standing in the couple's way if they were sure of each other's feelings, I was genuinely taken aback. All the more so when it was suggested that leadership was not my gift and it would be wise for me to hand the church over to others so that I could be free to teach and travel.

I did give the matter careful thought as, after all, the church was not my church. Jesus had said he would 'build [his] church' (Matthew 16:18) and I was just a very, very junior member of his construction team, being 'built in' myself while helping to build in others. I could also see that the leadership style I was trying to adopt at the time left me open to criticism from those who believed a 'first among equals' approach would be better than 'one among equals'. But in the few days that followed this confrontation, there were two separate occasions when God caused something to rise up in me to reject the handover.

With tensions building, I had no option but to warn the church, without naming names or giving away any of the background between myself and the person we'd been looking to, that we could be facing some challenges. I seriously overdramatised the announcement, borrowing words from Acts 27 and speaking of us hitting a sandbank and the ship breaking up while we all made it safely to land. The ship didn't break up (I certainly exaggerated that), but relationships did change when we reached the shore. There was no loss of life (in terms of spiritual life within the church), but we did lose some church members who preferred to settle elsewhere.

It was painful, but the experience wasn't wasted. Through it I came to see that there's a kind of fathering that can be more claustrophobic than liberating and more limiting than facilitating. I hadn't realised how important it is for elders to 'hold firmly to the trustworthy message as it has been taught'.[85] I can see now how wise it was for Paul to stress this in the similar list of eldership qualities he sent to Timothy.[86] There is no way that churches, especially those like ours with a focus on 'whole church' discipleship, can have one message being taught publicly and a different message being presented in private counselling sessions. The message has to stay the same. Church is no place for personal popularity campaigns. The last thing we need is competing visions, competing ideologies and competing parties all struggling for air-time.

It was good that things came to a head before we made another mistake. In our quest for more interpersonal and ministry-development space, we could have ended up being seriously cramped and conflicted. It was a good moment to reflect again on the last part of the sermon my friend preached at my baptism. The promise to the church in Philadelphia:

---

85. Titus 1:9.
86. 1 Timothy 3:1-7.

The one who is victorious I will make a pillar in the temple of my God. Never again will they leave it. I will write on them the name of my God and the name of the city of my God, the new Jerusalem, which is coming down out of heaven from my God; and I will also write on them my new name.

(Revelation 3:12)

Pillars are meant to stay put where they are and to fully identify with the place where they're committed. The great thing about the reward promised to the Philadelphian church was that nobody could be left in any doubt about who owned the pillar and where it belonged. It was owned by God the Father and Christ the Son, and belonged in the New Jerusalem Temple. It had three inscriptions on it to prove it. Pillars need to fully belong to where they are placed. Location marks are important. Experience gained elsewhere is not always instantly transferable. People who want to be seen as pillars in a church need to add to the church's unity and to act as role models, not as detractors.

There is one other thing I have noticed about pillars that I also believe applies to Church life. There are architects, and Wren was one of them, who see the value of using pillars to bring people in rather than just having them as part of the internal structure unseen by all who are outside. If you look at St Paul's Cathedral, it appears that Wren placed more pillars on the outside to hold up porches and attract people in than he put on the inside. I think this is a big lesson. We need to make sure that our inspirational and creative people can be seen. We still need them to be pillars, strong, stable and space-creating, and not just there for the show, but the things they create can be part of the outward face of the church. There are risks that go hand-in-hand with being profiled, and they are very different from the pressures that can come on those who are positioned to create space away from the public gaze. The creatives often make inspiring preachers, but a church still needs the hidden weight-bearers who can fulfil a one-to-one role encouraging and correcting those who need extra help to reach their potential.

When we moved into the community hall, we really had to prioritise our creatives and inspirers, as our outward-facing pillars. We were keen to play an open and effective part among the town's churches, and when we discovered that the hall had been built where three Anglican parishes meet, we talked to the vicars about how they would feel if we focused on 3,000 homes drawn from the corners of their assigned areas. With their support we then went on to speak to the local council about specific needs in the community, and got to know the schools, businesses, shops and medical practices, as well as the layout of the streets, the location of the blocks of flats and the whereabouts of sheltered housing and homes for the elderly. Once we'd done this, we carried out a swift church skills audit to put alongside our community findings to see which of the area's most pressing needs we were best able to meet. The lack of an after-school club for children came top of the list, and we let loose our most creative church members on this project to generate ideas and set up a programme.

To keep things in balance, we decided from the very beginning that we would still see our Sunday services as the major benefit we were bringing to the community. If most weeks visitors had been attracted to our home, we were confident that we would be welcoming even more visitors when gathering in a public space. No one had complained about our emphasis on Bible teaching, so we weren't going to change that either. We were definitely going to need strong internal pillars as well as creative and inspirational outward-facing ones.

We were learning that effective role models can really help in a church with a commitment to 'whole church' discipleship.

Question for reflection

How can we mobilise our church members to create the space required for individual growth while displaying the creativity needed to attract new people?

Chapter Nine: Still or Sparkling?

Eating out is not everyone's idea of fun. But even if you only do it occasionally, you may have noticed that in certain places asking for water to be brought to the table will open up a choice. If you insist, the person serving you will bring a jug of water from the tap, but more often than not you will be asked to choose between a bottle of sparkling and a bottle of still. Those who eat out regularly will instantly know which they prefer, but the truth is that if you pour out the sparkling and leave it standing long enough you probably won't be able to notice any difference. Sparkling water can lose its sparkle and some people's tastebuds seem to prefer it that way.

As someone who enjoys sparkling water, I would be tempted to make a case for tastebud re-education. With water it's of little consequence, but when a church loses its sparkle, it matters a whole lot more. No one stays in a restaurant long enough for the sparkling water to lose its sparkle, but a church is different. As the sparkle slowly goes, week by week, month by month, year by year, regular attenders may hardly notice the difference. Tastebuds are easily deceived and we are left thinking we still have the sparkle whereas in reality we've come to prefer church life when it's flat.

In the early part of the book, we talked about how and where to fit in. We now have to think about being the church that people will want to fit into. Pastoral care that respects and accepts is essential, and good role models make a huge difference, but if we've lost our initial drive, it'll be hard to keep anybody that comes our way who is brimming with energy or full of enthusiasm.

By the time we get to the book of Revelation there are several churches that have lost their spark, but Ephesus disappoints me most since it had such a great start.[87] Aquila and Priscilla faithfully prepared the way,[88] and Paul's amazing ministry in the school of Tyrannus, which impacted the whole region,[89] probably leading to the birth of the other six Aegean churches addressed in the book of Revelation.[90] There are, though, a few possible hints as to how the Ephesian church may have wandered away from its early passion. Luke records a conversation with the elders of the Ephesian church that Paul held along the coast at Miletus. After his time in Ephesus he'd moved on to Greece and now, maybe a year later, on his way back to Jerusalem, he's gathered them to encourage them and warn of tough times to come from false teachers.[91]

The second hint comes in the letters that Paul sent to Timothy when Timothy was based at Ephesus, perhaps some five or six years later. It seems that he and Paul had made a visit to the city after Paul's release (perhaps following on from Paul's visit to Crete with Titus). At the end of their previous time together in Ephesus, Paul had sent Timothy on to Macedonia,[92] but this time it's Paul who goes on to Macedonia and leaves Timothy to sort things out in Ephesus.[93] If this time-tabling is right, then some pretty radical restructuring is being recommended for Ephesus. The appointment of some fresh elders is on the agenda, to stand as role models, to strengthen the public Bible teaching in the city and to provide correction for church members who are being drawn off into false teaching.[94] What is telling is that Timothy seems to be at risk

---

87. Revelation 2:1-7.
88. Acts 18:19-28.
89. Acts 19:8-10.
90. Revelation 1:11.
91. Acts 20:17-38.
92. Acts 19:22.
93. 1 Timothy 1:3.
94. 1 Timothy 3:1-7; 4:13.

of not being taken seriously because of his age, and by this time, having been with Paul for maybe twelve years, he would at least have been in his early thirties.[95] Could this be a sign that ageism was creeping into the Ephesian church? If so, it was a really poor time for it to happen. When setting a church on a course where it's having to be wary of false teachers, the last thing one needs is for it also to become wary of younger voices. It sends out warning signals that the church is moving into a fortress mindset. Soon everything has to be checked, and caution, which has its place,[96] becomes the order of the day rather than life, joy and love.

These are pretty critical things to be suggesting about the church in Ephesus, and hopefully they are not reflected in churches that you and I know. But I am aware that when those who are role models start to feel anxious, it can lead to everyone feeling cramped, deadening the atmosphere in and around the church.

Many think that John wrote his first general letter soon after arriving in Ephesus. This could have been in the lead-up to the Jerusalem siege in AD 70. I am sure that if this is what he did, local believers would have been aware of what he was writing. In setting down his thoughts, he couldn't have been more fulsome about life, love and unity, but in summing up everyone's contribution to church life according to their level of development, he states something I'll never forget. When describing the young he wrote, 'You are strong, and the word of God lives in you, and you have overcome the evil one'.[97] Here are three qualities that no church can afford to miss out on. We all need them at the forefront of our congregations. And if we have a shortage of young people who are strong, Word-filled and victorious, we need to pray them in, raise them up, give them space and trust them enough to be our role models.

---

95. 1 Timothy 4:12.
96. Revelation 2:2.
97. 1 John 2:14.

We had only been meeting in the community hall for a few weeks when we had a fresh influx of university students, all keen to give their time and energy. They quickly involved themselves in the children's club, our house-to-house visiting, our summer outreach in the park, and a project where we'd converted a local shop into a youth centre. Fast forward a year or two, and as their university courses ended, many decided to stay on with us, finding accommodation in the area and eventually settling into family life among us. They were so central to the life of the church that we saw them as role models almost from the outset. They certainly had a way of attracting others in and making space for everyone to grow.

We hadn't forgotten, though, how important it was for Paul's church-planting strategy to have some pillars in place for everyone to look to.[98] We loved the idea of everyone growing together with plenty of room for all to develop their leadership abilities – increasing in responsibility and maturing relationally, while gaining some teaching, pastoral and evangelistic skills along the way. But to keep this going, we now needed more than ever those role models who totally embraced the vision and understood how to encourage and correct the ones who felt they needed special attention. Having a church vision that focuses on everyone being taken forward together is not without its challenges. Where there's a determination not to categorise people according to their needs, it's obviously important to have role models who can ensure the church's vision survives in the face of the expectations of those seeking extra attention. At the same time, it's essential to ensure that those requiring the extra attention can truly thrive in a church with such a vision.

Role models like this have to be willing to be hidden space creators, often having the kind of conversations behind the scenes that others would find it hard to handle. Few people realise how important it can

---

98. Galatians 2:9; Acts 14:23; Titus 1:5.

be for some church members to be given an explanation in private of what they've already heard in public. For some, these further conversations are a much-needed encouragement and for others, a necessary corrective. One-to-one teaching like this can be far more demanding than handling the public preaching from the platform or pulpit. It's an assignment that needs a lot of patience and grace. All the more so because these role models, who end up knowing more than anyone else about what is going on in the church, have to accept being consulted over every church plan and project. It is not a role that suits everybody.

Once we'd seen that appointing pillars 'Paul-style' was not about focusing in on age or profile, both of which we'd tried to major on in the past, it was easy to recognise three former students who were still in their twenties who'd been quietly developing eldership skills among us over a number of years. Furthermore, we could see that they would work well together. Everyone was consulted and everyone was happy about the choice. We had plenty of people in the church who were older and had more experience in church life, but everyone sensed that we'd found the people who would ensure unrestricted growth.

As you join us in breathing a sigh of relief at this point in our journey, do take note of how easy it is to skew the criteria for setting in place a church's role models. It's a tragedy to see churches ending up with appointments they regret as they watch their members become more and more inhibited. I think Timothy had a really difficult task in Ephesus, and I trust that in the end he wasn't hampered by those who looked down on him as too young and too inexperienced.[99] If our suggested timescale is right, it would be hard to think of anyone who had had more experience than Timothy.[100] It's worth us checking today where we might be setting our age and experience bar.

---

99. 1 Timothy 4:12.
100. Philippians 2:19-22.

Maybe as you've been reading this, Jesus' teaching on new wine and new wineskins has come to mind.[101] One of the points Jesus was making in using that picture was that his Church was not going to fit into the limitations of Moses' Law,[102] but like so many things that Jesus said it was a truth with a wider application. It is true that young leaders sometimes find it hard to fit into old systems; they are the new wine needing the new flexible wineskins that can expand with them. But what of the old wine that has already matured? It's tempting to think that it needs to be bottled, labelled and put on racks in special temperature-controlled cellars. In reality, though, since it no longer needs a flexible container to handle its early expansion, it can continue to mature anywhere. The young may need the new worship songs, the informality and less rigid service structures, but the mature should, and can, fit into these new expressions without the slightest risk.

Question for reflection

What steps can we take to avoid enthusiasm declining over time?

---

101. Luke 5:37-39.
102. Galatians 5:1,4.

Chapter Ten: A Bigger Picture

For someone like the apostle John, who'd been used to being at the centre of everything in Jerusalem,[103] the move to Ephesus must have felt like a disconnection.[104] But in moving west, John had no intention of being separated from the wider Christian world. Having written his letter to the churches at large soon after his arrival,[105] he set about increasing the sense of unity between the seven churches around the Aegean. Even when he ended up being taken as a prisoner to the island of Patmos, he had the seven churches on his mind.[106] He soon discovered that the risen Jesus had these churches on his mind too, bringing John a detailed message for each of them. The revelation he was given was full of pain and yet full of victory. It has since held out hope to the global Church for nearly 2,000 years.

The revelation began with John having to write down letters from Jesus to the seven Aegean churches. Two of these letters we've already mentioned,[107] but there is something that Jesus said to all seven that will set the mark for this chapter. To every single church he had John write, 'hear what the Spirit says to the churches'.[108]

There is a way of taking a picture with a laser that produces a three-dimensional effect. These pictures are called holograms and are used

---

103. Galatians 2:9.
104. John is believed to have spent the closing years of his life in Ephesus. This is backed up by his familiarity with the churches in the region and his exile on Patmos, which is a relatively nearby island.
105. Presumed dating of 1 John.
106. Revelation 1:9-11.
107. Revelation 2:1-7; 3:7-13.
108. Revelation 2:7,11,17,29; 3:6,13,22.

on our bank cards to stop counterfeiting. If you look at the small silvery square on the back of your card and move it around, you'll see that the image seems to change slightly and appears to have depth to it, even though the card is completely flat. Even if you were to cut the film holding the picture into hundreds of fragments, every single fragment, no matter how small, would carry the whole picture. Please don't try this on your bank card. Just type 'how holograms work' into your search engine. I've seen someone smash a glass hologram and hand out the fragments so I know it's true. It really is amazing. You would expect each fragment to have just the part of the picture that appeared on that piece of the film or glass when it was intact, but no, you get the whole picture every time.

When we become committed as Christians, we're immediately part of the Church at every level: locally, regionally, nationally and globally and, if we can get our heads around it, part of the Church right through history too, from the post-resurrection Pentecost to Christ's return and the new Jerusalem. That is the big, big picture and it's probably too big to hold in our minds. Yet whether we understand it or not, we are part of the whole, and each one of us individually contains all the characteristics of the biggest possible picture. But rather than start with the extremes of the largest and smallest, let's aim for somewhere in-between by thinking about how our local church is part of God's Church today, and build out the picture from there. Once we've done that, I'm sure we'll all be a whole lot clearer about just how big the big picture is, and we'll see a whole lot more about the Church Jesus is building.

So, let's start with our own local church and think what it looks like on a Monday morning. Sundays see us all gathered together, but Mondays see us all scattered. But we're still the church. We're the church in maybe 100-plus places: homes, schools, colleges, shops, offices, clinics, hospitals, laboratories, factories and workshops; and some of our retired members may be at clubs or social events. Us being the church might be a new thought to some, but it won't be new to many of those we meet and work with. When people meet us, they think they've met the church, often judging the whole Church on the impression they've formed of us. This may be daunting, but it's also exciting.

Between us, our local churches cover a wide area, and in all the places where we as members find ourselves, we carry the same hope, the same vision, the same love, the same joy, the same peace and the same liberty that we hold in church on a Sunday. We're the same people, wherever we are; fragments of the whole, but still carrying the whole. And if our local church is committed to turning followers of Jesus into leaders for Jesus, we will be bringing our sense of leadership responsibility with us too, with all of its graciousness and inclusiveness. We certainly found that this was the case for us in south London, and it hugely influenced our understanding of what it means to be an unstoppable church.

To build out our picture, we now have to scale up from our local church to the churches in our town or city. Being church members, we're automatically part of the Church at this level too. Some people love this thought so much that they prefer to think of the church as a town by town, or city by city entity, reflecting the way the New Testament refers to, say, 'the church of God in Corinth'.[109] This doesn't sit comfortably with those who think that the individual congregation is God's primary operational unit and the hub for all that God wants to achieve. To be honest, both arguments are unnecessarily restrictive.

The multiplicity of churches in our towns and cities today is something to rejoice about, not to weep over. Most towns and cities are of a size that requires more than one supermarket. So why not have multiple churches? And most people have a preferred supermarket they commit to, so what's wrong with being committed to a preferred church? The

109. 1 Corinthians 1:2; 2 Corinthians 1:1.

fact that churches are so different indicates both God's creativity and his wisdom. No two flowers look exactly the same, so why should any two churches have to be indistinguishable? No two people are the same, so why should they be faced with the folly of being forced into the same mould of church? I love the fact that God is so wise and creative. But that said, I know it's an incredibly powerful testimony when churches in a town or city work together, especially when this is done across a range of totally different church styles.

And we mustn't be put off when we discover that there are some projects that not all churches will want to engage in. The simple fact is that some initiatives require a greater level of doctrinal agreement than others. We just need to keep working with as many churches as possible on as much as possible, but do it without abandoning our commitment to being the church that we're called to be, with as much distinctiveness in our congregational make-up, conviction, style and practice that God's wisdom and creativity most certainly inspires. It's misleading to think that people will be helped or impressed by discovering that every church in town is exactly the same. It's better to surprise them by letting them see the love and respect that churches can show for each other.

So, scaling up to talk about church regionally, there certainly came a point for us when we as a church saw a significant shift in our thinking through our regional engagement. We registered for the first time that the size of events that can be put on regionally can change the spiritual climate in a way that builds confidence locally. The birth of the seven churches around the Aegean actually proved this. It seems that Paul's time spent teaching in the school of Tyrannus at Ephesus drew in people from the whole Aegean region,[110] including many who'd been caught up in a regional religious cult.[111] The impact of the gospel message

---

110. Acts 19:9-10.
111. Acts 19:23-27.

through this regional approach was extraordinary. No wonder there were other times in Paul's ministry when he planned regionally and strategically.[112] The south London event we became involved with as a lead-up to a capital-wide, stadium-based evangelistic campaign, not only led to new converts in the church but to levels of collaboration between churches that we'd never even dreamt of.

We now need to think about national Church, remembering that a lot of our press and broadcast news is at a national level, so this is where the Church has to make its impact in order to register in many people's consciousness. Participating at this level is not always easy, and it's tempting for church members to blindly follow the news media, taking on board the criticisms and comments of the press and then adding criticisms and comments of their own. Denominational coverage can be helpful, as denominations are often in a good position to gather information on the Church nationally, although not always across every denominational boundary. We owe it to our national Church leaders to support them in prayer and to avoid unresearched criticism, mindful of the eyes and ears of society, speaking up for them whenever we can.

As we move on to yet another stage, I also need to point out that we're not just looking at ever-widening circles of excitement and interest, but ever-widening circles of commitment. Each faces us with a challenge to gather information and pray; and also opens up possibilities of financial commitment. Jesus said, 'Where your treasure is, there your heart will be also' (Matthew 6:21), but the good news is that we're talking about giving joyfully and relationally rather than dutifully.[113] When you know people well and appreciate their needs, giving your time and attention can be much more meaningful than having the church treasurer send off a monthly subscription or subsidy.

---

112. Acts 16:10-12.
113. 2 Corinthians 9:7.

It amazes me how globally minded the Church was in New Testament times when it had no internet or phone system.[114] Compared with back then, we fall far short. I guess we had an advantage in our church in south London in that, at the time, Operation Mobilisation (OM), a large, energetic missionary movement, was running a number of its international projects from offices in our area. OM members frequently worshipped with us and some made our church their home. We had already taken the radical decision to define church as 'people we are making a commitment to' rather than 'people who have made a commitment to us', and working with OM pushed the boundaries of our understanding of this even further. We accepted that some people who were attracted to us might take time to settle. Those who were either unfamiliar with church or had set ideas about church needed time to weigh us up, but we never saw that as an excuse for taking undue time to commit to them. Our intention was to do this from day one, and to try to help them on their spiritual and personal journey in whatever way they wanted.

OM was certainly serious about mobilisation, and we never knew from one month to the next who out of those meeting with us might be going where. The good thing was that adjusting to these uncertainties worked wonders for our knowledge of what was happening in terms of Christian outreach around the world. And very quickly it wasn't just OM that was expanding our global thinking. Students coming from overseas to study in London were joining us and linking us up with their home nations, and some of our members were developing interest in other missionary societies too.

Having planted a church to prepare for missionary experience, Marion and I were realising we were in a church that was opening up missionary experience for others. We didn't just want to be a 'sending church',

---

114. Romans 16:1-15 shows Paul's familiarity with believers in Rome even before he had visited.

though, we wanted to be a 'going church', and that meant that we had to be prepared to travel too. One of our OM couples was being asked to relocate to Pakistan and as they left, I promised to visit them soon, not only to maintain the link with them as a family but to make sure that we as a church took the nation to heart in a way that would mean its challenges were going to be a major focus for us in the years ahead. Support would mean nothing if we were only going to be interested in those we sent, without being interested in the places we sent them, too.

My visits to Pakistan, and Marion's subsequent team visits to members serving overseas, helped our church set the pattern for the support we were seeking to give, regardless of which nation those who joined us might work in. We never saw ourselves as being the substitute for their chosen missionary society. We always welcomed the wisdom such organisations had gathered over the years and appreciated the need for them to take the lead. Even so, we considered it a massive privilege to be able to come alongside, to learn, to support, to give and to pray.

When Jesus had John write down the words 'hear what the Spirit says to the churches' he wasn't encouraging prying or gloating. He wasn't even saying, 'Have a look and see for yourself.' He was saying, in effect, 'I want you to hear how much I care for every church, regardless of its condition. You've seen how I'm prepared to stand with each one in wholehearted identification, and you've heard my congratulations and expressions of concern. You've listened to how I've introduced myself personally to each church and made church-specific offers of a victor's reward. Now, as you address your own issues, pray for them and stand with them that their light might burn brighter and brighter, as brightly as yours, so that the whole region becomes ablaze.'

If we all do this, can you imagine what the world will see? A global Church that really does reflect the glory of Jesus; the 'light of the world' (Matthew 5:14)!

Question for reflection

How can we help people appreciate their membership of the wider Church while fully benefiting from being part of their local church?

Chapter Eleven: A Movement, Not a Monument

When some countries go through regime change, their monuments to past rulers stand little chance of surviving. Excited crowds find ropes and tackle and pull the once-mighty down from their plinths, often to the sound of loud cheers, while amateur photographers capture the event in the hope of selling their videos to the world's media.

The Church has a lot of monuments that it's collected over the years, but as it's led by the risen Jesus, it's never going to face regime change. The important thing for the Church is that it must never see itself as a monument. Monuments are built with dead stones, but movements are built with living ones. The chances of creating a monument out of living stones are pretty much non-existent. It would be a monument that never stood still, recognisable as the Church but always reshaping. I would call that a movement rather than a monument, and it's the Church's greatest mission and joy to live up to these expectations and be a movement, not a monument.

What I've tried to show in this book is that the Church is alive and we need to allow its life to come to the fore. This will let its members grow as freely as possible. There's no point in ripping down Church systems and structures, whether they have been recently acquired or in place for centuries, if all we're going to do is to replace them with different ones in the hope of recreating some energy and enthusiasm. We have to work from an appreciation that the life is already there just waiting to be liberated. It's an understanding that comes from our grasp of

God's transformative good news. Ignorance of this could be our biggest problem. The resurrection life that God has given us is strong enough to break through, regardless of our systems and structures which, in the end, may not need changing at all.

Earlier in this book I shared a picture of the encouragement I got from seeing hidden bulbs break through and burst into flower in our drastically stripped-out garden. Where I worked as a dentist, my surgery overlooked two gardens, and when the neighbours who owned the further one decided to turn their home into a guesthouse, they made their garden into a car park. Throughout the autumn I watched them fell the trees and clear the ground to make it fit for its newly intended purpose. They then moved in the heavy machinery to put down a thick layer of asphalt. Instantly my view switched from attractive to functional. But a few months on, when the weather changed, I looked out on a black tarry surface covered with daffodils. The bulbs hadn't just broken through bare ground, they'd broken through the thick layer of asphalt.

Resurrection life is far more persistent than we might think, and today's 'fit for purpose' church needs to understand just how strong this life is. While we're busy trying to manage our members and keep them happy by maintaining the familiar, God has a different purpose that demands an alternative strategy. Jesus spelt it out for us: 'Every teacher of the law who has become a disciple in the kingdom of heaven is like the owner of a house who brings out of his storeroom new treasures as well as old' (Matthew 13:52). If that were true for the scribes back then, how much more true is it for us in our day? We really must make room for the new. We have to bring out the fresh as well as the familiar, and we can do this no matter how recent, or how ancient, our structures and systems might be.

In the end it's not about structures and systems, or even about size and simplicity, it's about a commitment to growth and togetherness.

Once we've grasped this, the structures and systems will usually prove adaptable enough to accommodate the upsurge of life, and flexible enough to facilitate the growth that will be coming our way. Small or large, simple or complex, it makes no difference. If we are prioritising growth and togetherness, God will make sure the life breaks through.

When we read what Peter wrote about living stones, we can feel the warmth with which he links up acceptance and togetherness: 'As you come to him, the living Stone – rejected by humans but chosen by God and precious to him – you also, like living stones, are being built into a spiritual house' (1 Peter 2:4-5). If Jesus as the foundation of this spiritual house has known rejection,[115] then those of us who come to him to be built into his house can be sure of his acceptance.[116] And that will apply no matter what we've experienced elsewhere. Peter clearly sees the Church as a welcoming Church where we can receive each other and grow together. But importantly he also sees the Church as a well-taught Church, writing of 'the things that have now been told you by those who have preached the gospel to you by the Holy Spirit sent from heaven' (1 Peter 1:12). The way he brings together preaching and the work of the Holy Spirit sits well with our quote from Jesus about the teacher of the law 'who … like the owner of a house brings out of his storeroom new treasures as well as old' (Matthew 13:52). We, as teachers of God's grace, need the Holy Spirit to inspire our preaching so we can bring out what is fresh without taking away from the familiar. Church is not just about being together, it's about continuing to *learn* together.

This is basic when it comes to embracing a 'whole church' discipleship approach. Peter addresses the Church by saying, 'Like newborn babies, crave pure spiritual milk, so that by it you may grow up in your salvation' (1 Peter 2:2). He expects us all to have healthy spiritual

---

115. 1 Peter 2:7; Psalm 118:22.
116. John 6:37.

appetites from the moment of our new birth, but we also need to add in John's understanding that the Church doesn't only contain spiritual children but spiritual youths and spiritual parents.[117] There's a need for those who teach to serve up spiritual meat as well as spiritual milk. The letter to the Hebrews puts it well: 'Anyone who lives on milk, being still an infant, is not acquainted with the teaching about righteousness. But solid food is for the mature, who by constant use have trained themselves to distinguish good from evil' (Hebrews 5:13-14).

We cannot afford to put everyone in our churches into the spiritual nursery. It might be convenient for the preachers and teachers who only have to prepare a five-minute homily, but we need to be aware that what we count as milk in our teaching today might not even have been considered as water in the New Testament Church. No wonder we see such slow personal growth. And how long before we wean people off the water onto the milk? And how long before we wean them off the milk onto the meat? We've had some people on the water and milk for so long that it's a wonder that their teeth haven't dropped out. Where is the training 'by constant use' that the writer to the Hebrews refers to? Paul taught all night in Troas and only one person, as far as we know, fell asleep, and that possibly could be put down to the heat of the lamps rather than Paul's preaching. Admittedly it had Paul dashing downstairs to rescue the young sleeper who'd fallen out of a window,[118] but in some of our churches it would probably be unwise to have anyone sitting by open windows if the preaching went on beyond twelve minutes.

I'm not suggesting that we go for length for length's sake; far from it, but preaching in the power of the Holy Spirit is never boring.[119] In many of our churches, some positive encouragement from us towards

---

117. 1 John 2:12-14.
118. Acts 20:7-11.
119. 1 Peter 1:12.

the preacher could lead to more prayer and more preparation, with far closer attention being paid to the congregation's spiritual progress. All of that would work wonders. We would soon have whole congregations capable of coping with a weekly mixture of milk and meat in a way that would see everyone's appetite (to say nothing of their chewing ability) steadily increasing.

I've tried to make sure this book follows the advice I've just given. In serving milk and meat I've wanted it to be both readable and practical. Every illustration, personal story and Bible narrative has been chosen with care so as to underscore each chapter's particular principle. There's nothing in this book that can't be applied in some way in every congregation, regardless of denomination. Some of you will appreciate the thought of going back to first-century Church growth principles, others will recognise the driving forces that led to the birth of your denomination; others will value the fact that you don't need to look back at all, but can start implementing these things from exactly where you are at right now.

If you're a church leader, you probably need to start by having a conversation with your leadership team, asking them how they see their roles. Peter offers a few comments that might be helpful to have at the back of your mind as you do this. He appeals to leaders as a fellow elder among them, urging them to serve willingly, and then adds 'not lording it over those entrusted to you, but being examples to the flock'.[120] I had a minister friend who began taking his church forward by having such a conversation with his elders and they found it so helpful – and if I recall rightly, such a relief – that it led to the transformation of his church.

If you're not in church leadership, and I expect that will be most of you, just remember that *you* are the church. As you keep building on your relationship with Jesus, you're already taking things forward.

---

120. 1 Peter 5:1-3.

The same is true as you keep on encouraging others, especially if at the same time you're recognising how much they're encouraging you. But there's much more to implementing this book's principles than that. If we want to see our churches providing great opportunities for learning and growing, both in terms of engaging with God and relating to one another, it's going to take serious commitment. It's great to have churches where people can open up to God in worship and prayer, but we also need our churches to be places where people can gain a better understanding of God through having the Bible opened up in a way that challenges and informs us. We can make this change happen, but it will take commitment. And what of pressing on to see our churches become places where every follower of Jesus becomes a leader for Jesus? That could be even more demanding, but that's precisely what becoming a follower who's also a leader is all about. It means taking responsibility and being willing to step ahead. Taking a lead in church doesn't make you the church leader, but as you step out it will equip you to take responsibility in your workplace, home and community too.

I had to learn all of this in south London where God led me to make a commitment to a church which had a culture that was totally unfamiliar to me except for a few similarities with my university Christian Union. This transition was unusual; God certainly doesn't expect all of us to plunge ourselves into an unfamiliar culture. Sometimes he immerses us into a very familiar culture with a commitment to help bring growth and change. One thing is certain, and that is that lasting growth and lasting change have to come from within. I found myself in a church that seemed to have the right ingredients for growth but was waiting to grow. I was there to learn and to contribute to the expansion.

We all want our churches to be places where growth is the goal. Churches may talk about putting on discipleship programmes to encourage personal development, but I learned that our churches themselves are God's perfect discipleship programme, his amazing one-size-fits-all growth and development experience not to be missed. If you keep God's aim in mind, it'll save you from a lot of discouragement.

It was a great help when I stepped into church leadership to have people around me who shared my enthusiasm. We all wanted to strengthen our relationship with Jesus and with one another, and we were all keen to make an impact for God's kingdom wherever we happened to be. It was that sense of togetherness that kept me well away from any kind of leadership pedestal and made sure that I continued to see every one of us as living stones being built into God's living church.[121] Even when newcomers were wondering whether or not to deepen their commitment to us, I found myself strengthening my commitment to them, valuing them and wanting them to grow. So much so that if it turned out that we weren't going to be the best fit for them, it simply challenged us to do more to increase the warmth and welcome of our church and its 'whole church' discipleship approach.

Obviously, if you're a church leader, you'll have to accept that I don't know exactly where you are at on your journey, but I can assure you that no matter the size, age or diversity of your congregation, the fact that you are part of it is an astounding gift to you from the Lord Jesus, so you need to love and value every member. I realise that you'll get to know some better than others, and there's nothing wrong with that, but make sure everyone feels appreciated. Work on creating a culture where everyone is respected by all, accepted by all, and is never at risk from having their needs exposed to all. Lift your eyes above the problems that crop up (and there will definitely be some – face them as challenges designed to help you grow) and see the leadership potential in every single member, even if it takes an effort – with some you have to see it by faith. It'll be a tremendous encouragement for you to have this kind

121. 1 Peter 2:5.

of thinking at the front of your mind. It will change your perspective on Church.

The truth is that we all need to see ourselves as leaders among leaders. When it comes to Church, you may be an ordained leader among non-ordained leaders, but just recognise that some who are not formally ordained by the wider Church can still be ordained by God.[122] Just enjoy the fact that there's no need for you to feel alone. Forget about being looked up to, and revel in the fun of having people alongside you who love you and respect you and who, in their different ways and at different levels, will be sharing the load.

We must go forward together, breaking down every hint of that monumental Church that people have conjured up in their minds. We must get rid of their imaginary plinth and their concretising of history and create a great mobilisation that leaves even the most sceptical person gazing open-mouthed.

Now, back to our builder from Chapter One who was taken by surprise when the living stones began to disrupt his neatly ordered wall. Imagine if he'd kept on building. He would have had surprise after surprise. The wall would have kept on growing, but he would have seen stones adjusting to accommodate each other's evolving design. He would have discovered that the wall could come under pressure, fracturing some stones and deforming others, and yet as he waited, he would have seen each stone recover to be stronger and better able to carry the weight than before. All of this would have taken our builder by surprise, but none of it has ever taken Jesus by surprise. He's always intended to build his Church this way, not just as a single wall but as a house with pillars and porches, designed for spaciousness and yet with every part of the structure securely in place.[123] He knows how to make us fit together and

---

122. John 15:16. KJV uses 'ordained'.
123. Proverbs 9:1.

to recover from the knockbacks.[124] He knows how to heal the broken and restore the wounded.[125] He knows how to turn his followers into leaders who can carry responsibility in the Church and in the world at large.[126] He knows us through and through and values each one of us,[127] not only as a living stone, but as a precious stone.[128]

Jesus has been building his Church through the centuries. We see his handiwork throughout the book of Acts, bringing people together and creating local congregations where people could grow freely in their relationship with him. We see it throughout history, when men and women have stepped out afresh, surrounded by like-minded believers, longing for the world to see in their day the transforming relevance of an unstoppable church. And what of today? All the ingredients are there. The resurrection life of Jesus is still the same, so why should our structures and systems be barriers to breakthrough? We need to prioritise his life, coming together as living stones so that we can keep on growing.

Let's make this happen so that today's world can experience the irresistible momentum of God's *Unstoppable Church*.

Question for reflection

How can the ideas shared in this book help your church, and the global Church, maintain its momentum?

---

124. Ephesians 4:14-16.
125. Psalm 147:3.
126. Matthew 10:16.
127. Psalm 139:1-6.
128. 1 Peter 2:5; Malachi 3:17.